For Ann

with love LB.

C000069339

THE EXTRA MILE

THE EXTRA MILE

Fifty Years in the Healing Ministry:
a Biography of Noel Wynyard

Tessa Kuin Lawton

The Book Guild Ltd
Sussex, England

First published in Great Britain in 2002 by
The Book Guild Ltd
25 High Street,
Lewes, East Sussex
BN7 2LU

Typesetting in Perpetua by
Keyboard Services, Luton, Bedfordshire

Printed in Great Britain by
Bookcraft (Bath) Ltd, Avon

A catalogue record for this book is available from
The British Library

ISBN 1 85776 662 8

Earth's crammed with heaven,
And every common bush afire with God;
But only he who sees, takes off his shoes,
The rest sit round it and pluck blackberries.

Elizabeth Barrett Browning (1806–1861)
(*Aurora Leigh*)

CONTENTS

ACKNOWLEDGEMENTS

I would like to thank the following people for their time and kindness in helping to collate the necessary material for this book:

Mrs Rosemary Armour; The Revd Michael Burden (General Secretary, The Guild of St Raphael); Sister Christine SLG (Sister in Charge of SLG Press, Fairacres); The Revd Hugh Dickinson (former Dean, Salisbury Cathedral); Miss Suzanne Eward (Librarian and Keeper of the Muniments, Salisbury Cathedral); Robin Howard (Editor of British Society of Dowsers Journal); Sister Isabel Mary, SLG; Marie Jelley (Secretary, The Churches' Council for Health and Healing); The Revd Robert Llewellyn (Julian Shrine, Norwich); Sister Mary Magdelene, SLG; The Revd David Slater (former Vicar of the Close, Salisbury); Margaret Turner (Church House, Salisbury); Alison Milne; Lisa Johnson.

FOREWORD

Healing is an emotive and complex subject. This book does not set out to explain it, nor does it expect to understand it. Contained here is an account of one woman's experience and the impact it had on her life and faith. As part of the account, reference must be made to the miraculous; but this is no catalogue of such events. Part of the complexity of the subject is to render the ordinary more often miraculous than the extraordinary. The total commitment of the 'one-to-one' ministry brought Noel in touch with the full depth of human distress and illness. From the start, her ministry was centred on those who felt they had been abandoned; by their families, the church, the medical profession. She shared the sufferings of these people with gratitude, whilst experiencing the dignity of their need in day-to-day contact.

LONDON

1

THE SILENCE

. . . Put off the shoes from your feet, for the place on which you are standing is holy ground.

Exodus 3:5

Religion grips people in different ways. A few are lucky enough to be struck by visions of God which can be neither denied nor ignored. Many have a creeping awareness that the life they lead is not exactly what it might be. The vast majority have a head full of questions; questions for which answers are required before they can give rational assent to something locked in an emotional subconscious. But amid the busy clatter of the logical is a proposition which is too rarely offered for consideration; which is a pity, because its simplicity may be beguiling enough to make people stumble into the belief for which they yearn.

Locked in the caverns of the mundane, every human has the capacity and the desire for space; a quiet beauty, a small personal retreat, in which to express considered truths about the self, unconstrained by circumstance. A place to be, where shrill thoughts dissipate in the ether of attention. To accept the truth of this proposition is but one step away from believing that such silence could be found through waiting. To wait requires no renunciation of rationality, only the stilling of its noise; and perhaps the belief that the goal is worth the process.

In 1950 the noise of Westminster and Fleet Street had

3

crowded in on one woman to the point where her mind could no longer breathe. As editor of a contemporary political journal, she could not allow her mind to be starved of air and so, to sharpen it up, she created an opening for herself. Each week she walked the grey streets to St Mary's Church, Bourne Street and pushed open the doors to the vast interior. Vaulted ceilings gave her room to stretch into the dark silence, and she sat. And listened.

She identified the voices of her child and dead husband. She acknowledged the voices of survival and pride as they tried hard to mask pain and cover vulnerability, and was suddenly faced with a wilderness of empty silence. She turned, to remind herself from where she had come, and her eye was distracted by horizons on which she could not focus. To have discovered this plain of emptiness within herself was a revelation.

This was how it had begun. The realisation of the space within. In time this retreat became increasingly important. Her attention was fixed by anything which resonated with this discovery of silence. The journal was a passport to some extraordinary people and she now included the religious among her interests; spending as much time in the echoing caverns of cathedrals as in the lobby at Westminster. It does not take a university education to train a mind in the art of investigative research; only an active intelligence and an unquenchable thirst for information. Noel Wynyard had discovered that the way to learn was to combine the knowledge of the wordsmith with the insights of an effective interview. Two talents had equipped her with all the credentials she required: an ability to read 'like the wind' and an intuitive understanding of people. Like a gifted confessor she had been graced with the virtue of discretion and the patience to listen. Very few knew what she thought or felt, even those closest to her; but her aptly-timed questions and a refusal to be shocked drew out the most intimate considerations from, as she put it, 'char to head of state'.

She had changed her name soon after the war, when she returned to London to pick up the debris of her life. It was a strong name resonant with the inheritance of a literary

4

family. The ambiguity of Noel granted her interviews with members of some of the most exclusive men's clubs. In the aftermath of World War II, a time of chaotic freedom when the entrepreneur held all the aces, she banished the past and protected herself with the determination to survive. The war had crumbled the rigid framework of British propriety and this elegant single mother in her well-cut trouser suits and jaunty hats strode into Fleet Street to take her place among the seasoned hacks; her only credentials were a discredited letter of introduction from an Australian newspaper and a war history in Pacific Intelligence. Her managing editor in Australia may have failed her, but by using the same initiative which had promoted her in six months to his associate editor on *The Melbourne Argus* she walked the streets of Whitehall and raised enough capital for a new quarterly journal. *Life Line* would set out to document current affairs and post-war thought.

Noel had worked as a freelance reporter for all the main dailies until two friends, who ran a small business selling leading articles to the press, offered her the use of an office in Parliament Square, in return for the job of lobby correspondent in the House of Commons. Every day, Noel had to read *Hansard*, decide which debates to attend and then write up her account of proceedings. She became well known among MPs and respected for the even-handed way in which she dealt with issues and individuals. Her conversations and discussions with many of the leading politicians of the day stood her in good stead as she planned her new journal.

For five years it was effectively a one-woman show while she cut back her work in the House of Commons: the arranging of interviews, organisation of guest writers, editing, photography, planning and layout. She also ran a house and brought up a young child. Despite attracting excellent reviews and distinguished contributors, the journal's long-term future was permanently in jeopardy as people refused to shake off the shackles of their wartime subsistence living. Financial worries added themselves to a catalogue of problems from which there was little escape. And yet, at St Mary's she had discovered this well of tranquillity.

5

Had it not been uncovered in a church she might not have connected its existence to God. It may be that without the fragile example of her parents' Sunday faith she would never have placed it within the framework of Christianity. Indeed her brushes with the Christian establishment thus far meant that her initial reaction was to shy away from all contact with the religious. But the presence of a lone priest at the church became, after many visits, a reassurance. From there, the step to conversation was not so great.

Father Patrick confirmed her sense of wonder and began to explain the nature of faith. He talked to her of grace and discernment. Somehow it had never occurred to her that God might take the initiative; she had always thought that since Eden the ball was placed firmly in the human court. From the Fall onwards the bond had been broken and God had floated far out of reach, a distant and disgruntled parent whose very power and omniscience demanded recognition and appeasement. No-one had ever talked to her about the beauty of God, the inspiration of a Creator who infused the earth with colour and encouraged an encore from its resources with every renewed season. With millions of others, Noel had drawn strength from these things but had never connected the peace they gave her with the quiet in her soul. The very acknowledgement of this was enough to open her eyes and give her the confidence to marvel at the immanence of God. She realised that the silence within was not tied to St Mary's but was something she carried around with her and to which she had permanent access. Father Patrick taught her how to tap into it each day by creating physical space for herself and resting in it. He called it waiting: not waiting *for* anything, but waiting on the silence. Or *in* it, if she preferred. And she began to find the time each day to be alone. Little by little she was discovering a new energy; a steady stream of life filling her waking hours. Her determination in the face of the storm relaxed more often into a smile — and still she survived. The battle with time no longer left her shaken, it stretched to accommodate her. The dark fears which tormented her broken nights were less rebellious; she had even dared to glance at them. It was not a contentment, nor an ease which she felt. Her soul was no more at peace than it had been the previous year. But her time at St Mary's had rekindled in her a sense of hope.

Her conversations with Father Patrick allowed her to talk frankly about her understanding of religious matters in a way she had never been able to before. In lowered tones, on a hard wooden pew, they would explore the images of God she had accumulated and watch how they fared in the filtered light of their scrutiny. He did not tell her what to believe but listened as she investigated the nature of her long-held beliefs, and encouraged her to recognise and name the fear of a two-dimensional life as faith. It seemed a simple starting point and her confidence to talk about such matters grew.

It occurred to her that the God she believed in was concerned primarily with dictating moral absolutes. She called God 'Father' but feared and mistrusted Him: the war had taught her that He was not only distant but capricious. It shook her to realise that this God did not correspond to long held beliefs about 'good' and 'love'. And so the priest asked her to talk of love. Most people can talk about love: even if the picture is barely recognisable in their own life. The pain of loss dissipated when conversation turned to her child. The more she talked, the more she became aware of the discrepancy between her own relationship with her child and the way she approached her Father. The title, as a relationship, was devoid of meaning. Had God always loved her? Had He always been there? She felt cowed in the face of appalling memories of torture during the war, of death and betrayal. God had been there, as judge and jury, observing from a distance as His Creation mutilated and destroyed itself; voyeuristic, unmoved in the face of the depths of human tragedy. He had set down the rules. They had been spectacularly broken. Could one expect anything else?

The priest made her notice that God *had* been part of the horror, but then moved her quickly on. There was too much there to haunt and immobilise the spirit. So he talked instead of beauty. Noel Wynyard understood beauty. The priest directed her to its presence in her own life: in every photo she took, in the surprising proportions which jostled into composition before her critical eye, in the faces which hurried through her life in every street, and the fine lines of architecture. Perhaps, most of all, in the countryside — she would long for an assignment in the country, searching out any rural story which might touch upon the fast pace of a self-concerned capital. In the movement of the willow, the curve of the landscape, she had no problem seeing love and recognising the Creator's touch. Realising the door which this opened for her, she started travelling regularly to Dorset, where so much of her youth had been spent. On the pretext of photographic assignments she would walk, immersing herself in the scenery. Here her intellect was not engaged and her heart was lifted simply by breathing the air. She no longer felt alienated, but somehow at one with the undercurrent of life. It was possible to imagine here that the Creator and created were in relationship with one another and it was a relationship of which she could feel a part. Her visits here restored her to wholeness and gave her the strength to cope with the City.

2

FRANCISCAN ASPIRANT

Who shall ascend the hill of the Lord? And who shall stand in his Holy place?

Psalms 24:3

It was soon after one such visit that the priest at St Mary's, Bourne Street, mentioned to Noel the possibility of a retreat. Father Patrick had contacted the Abbess of the Benedictine community of St Mary at Malling, asking particularly that Noel be taken under her wing. He knew the Abbess Mary as forthright; someone who would understand both Noel's scepticism and intelligence.

As a child, she had visited the Franciscan monastery at Hilfield, Dorset, as her mother's apprentice. Known locally for their remarkable weaving ability, the Irwin children were taught to respect those who lived 'on the Lord's favour'. Everilda Irwin had no great faith of her own but respected the place of the monastery in society as intercessor on behalf of people like her. Such people deserved to be assisted wherever possible, and within such an environment one could learn important lessons about life. So, when Noel showed an interest her mother began to take her to Hilfield for open days; and would occasionally replace the local parish service with a visit to the Franciscan chapel. The monks appreciated her desire to introduce the child to their way of life and suggested that perhaps Noel might help them in their mission to equip those wayfarers who passed through their doors with a skill which they could offer in employment. And so she would travel regularly through the narrow lanes of Dorset to the monastery to offer her weaving talents to the community. The stark contrast of the complete tranquillity of the house and chapel, with the confusion and disorientation of the people with whom she worked, was one which would never leave her. It was an uneasy alliance, but it seemed to her to be the matter of every soul. She saw it within herself, and in all those around her. With her mother's idealism she could never believe that this tension was also inherent in the life of the professionally religious. Her faith in authority, passed down so effectively from her mother, meant that there was always a screen drawn between the religious and the mortal. That was the way that it should be; the natural order of things. Like her mother, she assumed that talent and presence were worldly qualities that had no use in and of themselves, but could perhaps gain some merit by being put at the disposal of those who knew God. Her contact with the monastery became, therefore, her spiritual life by proxy. It was years later that she realised that the contentment of walking through the countryside, the union of her spirit with the natural world, as well as the soaring heights that her spirit reached when listening to chapel plainsong were in fact the essence of her *own* spiritual life. Nor did she comprehend the connection between the worth she felt in sharing a talent (and equipping someone with the tools of independence) and the God of whom the Gospels spoke. But all these experiences sowed the seeds, and may even have fed her soul, in the dark years that lay ahead.

On her return from Asia with a small child, she had settled in London, believing it to be a place where one could slip into anonymity among a host of similarly displaced people. Here was an England which offered her all the familiarity for which she had been homesick, but none of the comfort. That had not troubled her at first. 'Living through a war does not lead one to expect comfort,' she said. Noel had not returned for peace of mind, but because she could think of nowhere else to go. A return to the country was impossible: she had changed too

10

much to pick up the threads of her previous life. But at least in London she was back at the heart of operations and connected once more with 'HQ'. The world of politics and diplomacy was the only one where the language felt familiar. Stationed in Australia, her work in intelligence and journalism had meant daily connection with London and the heart of the war communications office. It had been her lifeline; the customs and formalities a thin thread of normality in an otherwise insane world. It gave her a framework within which to understand herself; and when her life crumbled, that structure was just rigid enough to keep her from falling. Immersed in a city which was as foreign as it was well known, she reached for the lifeline again and began to pursue the contacts she had made from the other side of the world. With her daughter Caroline installed in school, she began the lengthy process of uncovering the enclosed world of politicians and war personnel and decoding the secret language and network that was theirs. Fired by loyalty to those whose lives she had shared in Asia, and certain of the need of those Commonwealth countries to remain connected to Britain in the aftermath of the war, she had set up *Life Line* – the journal which was to 'document contemporary thought'. This was her answer to a very close encounter with war. After five years in Australia she was convinced that the British Empire was essential. In this journal she hoped to champion the causes of sanity, civilisation and humanity during 'the state of world chaos which all thinking people recognise as temporarily inescapable after two world wars'.[1]

Her work in Whitehall allowed her to walk the streets of a world she knew in an otherwise hostile environment. But she still yearned for the contentment she had felt as a child before the war had turned her life upside down, even before she had met Donald and travelled with him to a new life in Asia. She knew she could not return to Dorset, but her spirit yearned for rest, so she turned to the only religious institution she had ever known.

The monks at Hilfield welcomed her enquiry and wrote at length suggesting possible courses of direction. Matters of faith had always been black and white for Noel and her desire for ease of spirit was so great that she determined to take the most arduous path of all for a lay person: the Franciscan Third Order. To the woman for whom nothing had ever come easily, it seemed right that peace of mind should only come about through discipline and hardship. She did not believe that she could ever really be like them, the disparity between the laity and the religious had been so strongly instilled in her by her mother; but she wanted to recapture the peace she had known through giving her talents to them, and this was the only way she could think of.

At that time an aspirant for the Franciscan Third Order was obliged to undertake spiritual direction, as well as keeping to a strict and carefully planned rule of life. Such spiritual discipline was hard even for the settled man; for a single mother and sole breadwinner it was nearly impossible. But she believed that it was the means by which she might overcome the tragedy of her past and recapture the contentment of a childhood vision. So she incorporated the rule into her hectic life and found time to travel to Godalming once a month for spiritual direction under Reginald Somerset Ward. A priest used by the Franciscans as Spiritual Director for their aspirants, he was a man renowned for his vigorous and sometimes eccentric discipline. And it was here that the emphasis lay. Discipline. Obedience to the commands of God. He taught her the rudiments of prayer, always stressing the importance of military-precision timing and regularity. It was a method she could understand and relate to: it made absolute sense that God should be as strict as the senior levels of the Secret Service in His requirements of time-keeping and order! Father Ward would instruct her in the art of forgetting self; of seeing only the higher goal. It was not that God required the penance of wearing her hat backwards in the press gallery of both Houses in Parliament, nor that he desired her to go without make-up to every interview she conducted on a Friday, but rather that she should be aware of the unimportance of such matters. Such instruction did not always achieve its aim: it took a very long time indeed to overcome the self-consciousness which such action induced, and even longer before she could move on to indifference about such worldly concerns as fashion and appearance. But perhaps that in itself was a lesson.

At the end of every three months Father Ward was expected to write a report to the Franciscans about the progress of their aspirant. Based on her ability to keep the rule and the way in which this was helping her spiritually, the report included a small section which Noel herself had to write. It was not theologically challenging, simply asking her to confirm what her director had written. After two years of working with Father Ward, the Order brought to his attention her record of books read. This was a list of books which she took upon herself to read after recommendation from her director. Each book was recorded and summarised. The list was checked every quarter before the report was written to the Friars. At each meeting she and her director would discuss some of the material she had read and the way in which she had incorporated it into her life. It had not taken long, however, for Father Ward to become frustrated at the shortage of time he had with her. Her brain was quick and her capacity for understanding and interpreting some of the most profound theological and spiritual works, surprising. He tried to keep up with the material that she read, but found it increasingly hard to do so. He suggested to the Franciscans that he be allowed to have more time with Noel, but was refused permission. She herself had been unsure about the demands on her time which further journeys out of town would entail. If she were honest with herself, she got more out of reading the books he recommended than from the visits to Godalming. In this way she could escape into the realms of the intellect and the silent spaces of prayer, rather than confront the nature of her faith. Reading was something she did well: as a reviewer for *The Times Literary Supplement* she read several books a week and could digest them for succinct summary in a matter of hours. This talent allowed her to make a small living when she first arrived in London, and was something of which she was quietly proud. It was no surprise to her that it had also become a refuge.

13

Imagine then her shock when the man of God in whom she had put her trust accused her one day of lying. He had been compiling the material for her eighth quarterly report and reviewing the list of books she had been keeping, and now challenged her that the list she kept was more fantasy than fact. Unable to believe what he was saying, she simply repeated that she had read all these and reviewed them; without attempting to justify herself.

This incident was marked on her report and taken up for questioning by the friars when they came to consider her as an oblate. When they too questioned her integrity, her faith in the authority of the religious was so damaged that she signed herself off: not even acknowledging their careful suggestion that she should undertake another year of probation before joining. Her understanding of the structures of religious authority had never progressed beyond a childhood acceptance that all men of God were like saints. Her most recent experience in Asia had acquainted her with human fallibility and weakness, yet she had clung to the notion that there walked on earth those who were not touched by this; those who knew the secret of goodness and truth. That these people might be human too, was something she did not care to acknowledge; for then she would have no-one left to guide her and no-one to look to for inspiration.

For the duration of Father Ward's direction she had managed to avoid the subject of her faith. They had talked of theology and of politics and she had emulated his own quiet certainty. But her ability to keep her beliefs private had discouraged him from broaching the subject of her faith too explicitly. He had indulged her thirst for knowledge and discussion, and had become more of a tutor to her than director. He was aware of this, but believed it to be the right way forward for one as private as herself. Surely it was impossible to have the kind of academic conversations they enjoyed and not to be moved to ask profound questions of one's faith? What he had not done, however, was to supply her with the tools to ask such questions. She had never understood faith as experience, only as an intellectual assent to a distant reality. He, meanwhile, had hoped that the tools of the intellect would help her to unlock the spirit. He waited for her to open up to him, while she had drawn strength from the academic nature of their relationship and remained happy to believe that this was all that was required of her.

Father Ward had been taken in by her apparent confidence and assurance. He could not have believed that her faith in his authority was absolute; he talked with her as if with an equal. His query about the quantity of books she read had seemed to him innocuous, and his comment on the subject had been intended as a witty reflection on her tendency for hyperbole. He had misread her entirely, and was at a loss as to how to repair the situation when her rejection from the Franciscans came through. To his shame, he was paralysed by embarrassment and did not contact her again.

Far from having advanced along a spiritual path, Noel's beliefs about God were as static as they had ever been. The confusion of authority and power, coupled with the response of discipline and obedience, had now become a tangled mess which only ostracised her further from the faith she had known as a child. She had arrived in London as a virtual stranger in her own country. Apart from her child, she had nothing. She had tried, methodically, to build up a web of contacts and establish for herself a foothold in society. But London did not allow you to put down roots. Her time with the Franciscans and Father Ward had been a time of solace and some refuge. Now that her contacts with them had been cut, she found herself in danger of being overwhelmed by the demands of her life in London.

3

BENEDICTINE OBLATE

*I made known to them thy name, and I will make it known, that
the love with which thou has loved me may be in them, and I
in them.*

John 17:26

Even at her lowest ebb, Noel did not realise that the energy
to continue with her work was a gift from God. Nor that the
inspiration she received from her *Life Line* was the energy of
the Spirit. It took her many years to connect this energy and
inspiration with her own determination to survive. At the time
it was merely a disjointed sequence of events, not even understood for their sustaining qualities, although she was dimly
aware that in spite of it all she had never yet 'gone under'.

And now she was presented with another opportunity:
Father Patrick had arranged for her to go on retreat to a
Benedictine convent. She had not charted the gradual move
back from the fringes of the Church, but the step which this
priest was now asking her to make seemed less difficult than
she might have expected. Only now did she realise the extent
of involvement which the sacraments of silence and friendship
had drawn from her. She acknowledged the duplicity of kindness and was grateful to Father Patrick. Perhaps the greatest
gift the Lord had given her was the ability to trust again in
the face of betrayal. To accept the offer of a retreat seemed a
fitting way to repay him.

Founded in 1891, the convent at Malling was an enclosed order of Benedictine nuns dedicated to silent prayer and contemplative intercession. One of the first Anglican orders for women, it had revolutionised the way in which the Church had understood prayer. No longer an added extra which one hastily skipped over during the Sunday service, the convent propagated the need for careful instruction about prayer and a renewed sense of its power and importance.

In all their conversations, Father Patrick had never pushed Noel to talk of prayer. They had shared times of quiet together but he had chosen not to interrupt such times by attempting to articulate what was going on. She had never spoken of her faith, nor of her previous experience with the Church, but the time now seemed right to mention a retreat at Malling. He knew that she had a barrage of questions about her own faith, which in the right situation she would form, and with the right person to draw them out of her, she might voice. Most importantly, he knew that her experiences of God must be recognised for what they were, so that she might begin to build on them and incorporate them into her own life. He had a sense that God was preparing her for something but that she had not yet fully recognised that it was God who was talking to her. That was the first step: to discern the voice and to have the courage to converse. He hoped that Mother Mary would give her the tools.

The scale of the fear which Noel felt on entering the interview room was matched only by the curiosity of stepping into a fully enclosed order. The room was large and white; utterly bare apart from a gold icon on the wall and the wooden panel and grille which separated her from the Abbess. She was called over to the bench beside the grille and so began her interview. To her surprise the Abbess began by asking what she wanted from the next few days; and Noel found that from the start she had to do the thinking for herself. Not knowing what to ask for, she told the Abbess of her discovery of St Mary's Church and of her dissatisfaction with her life in London. She began to talk about the importance of the silence in her life and the chance which Malling offered her to draw deeply from that well. Mother Mary outlined the pattern of the week ahead and gave her directions to her room, before withdrawing and leaving Noel alone.

Over the course of the week the Abbess showed herself to be a person who could explain to Noel the scope of the journey and give some idea of the way ahead. She had not taken the place of Father Ward, nor healed the wounds of Hilfield, but taught Noel what it was to lead *herself* along the path. Mother Mary had shown Noel how to draw on what was within her. She had not been embarrassed to talk of God, and did so in such an easy way as to make it quite natural for them both to discuss it together. She had traced the journey of Noel's faith and in so doing had brought into focus the many experiences of her past. She realised that she had 'home' within her and could therefore never be ostracised again. This astonishing revelation was completed when, back in the white room once more for her final interview, the Abbess suggested that Noel become an oblate of the Order. There was no lengthy training or testing period. From that moment on, Noel became Sister Prisca and joyfully bent her will to a new rule of life which demanded the reading of seven offices a day and regular contact with the convent.

She knew that her time in London was now drawing to a close, although she did not know how long this signing off would take. She could not see that her journal would never print its fourteenth issue, but she knew that setting it up had been enough. It was not that she had any clear sense of direction or knowledge of her future, only that each day was leading her to somewhere yet unknown and that London had been a stepping-stone. She became increasingly interested in the life of the religious, and pressed Father Patrick for news of speakers or conferences which she might attend. Thus she went to hear Brother Edward at Holy Trinity, Sloane Square, and later Archbishop Anthony Bloom, Archimandrite of the Orthodox Church. The former was the founder of the Village Evangelists, a group which set out to visit every parish in England, spreading the message of the living God. Captivated by his face, Noel went up to speak to Edward after the

18

service. In the short time during which they spoke, she felt that there was a meeting of minds. He asked her for her name and she told him she was Sister Prisca, an oblate of Malling. It was all the information he needed to remember her by.

When she went to listen to the young Orthodox Archbishop, she was utterly drawn into every word he said. 'It is unusual,' he later remarked, 'to come across someone who is not only listening to every word you say, but living it in spirit.' When preaching, he picked her out from the congregation and found himself speaking almost exclusively to her. When she met him afterwards they felt as if they already knew one another, and talked like old friends. He introduced her to the spirituality of the Orthodox Church, recommending the ancient Philokalia[2] and the recently published works of Iulia de Beausobre[3]. It was the beginning of a long-lasting friendship.

In 1951 the opportunity to heal the open wound of her relationship with the Franciscans was offered in a chance reunion with Sister Mary McCulloch. Noel had first met Sister Mary at Hilfield, on retreat, and the two had become firm friends. Mary was a UMCA[4] missionary who had been posted to Nyasaland soon after the two had met. They had kept in touch by letter, although their correspondence had gradually fallen away after Noel's rejection from the Third Order. Yet here was Mary, in the middle of Piccadilly, looking as though she hadn't had a decent meal for several weeks! Noel gathered her up and took her back to her house in Chelsea, where she determined she should stay until she had recovered. They talked at length about the plight of returning missionaries and Noel offered her the use of the house whenever she came back to England from Africa. In this way she would have somewhere to base herself where she could collect her thoughts and gently make the transition back to the English way of life. With Caroline at school, the house was empty for the better part of the day; and despite rather cramped conditions, guests were always welcomed. Mary was deeply grateful to her friend and wondered at the transformation which had taken place in her.

They talked at length about the religious life and all it had to offer: about the vast reservoir of untapped energy among the laity. Mary talked of the frustrations and joys of the missionary life and the fresh perspective on the Church which sharing the Gospel in another culture gave. She blessed Noel for her gift of listening and loved her for her real interest in Africa, its peoples and culture. Over the course of two months she shared every hope and plan, every dashed dream and abandoned prayer with her friend. They put the world to rights over a late night bottle of wine, and the Church to rights at every morning prayer. But most importantly they hatched a plan for the future.

Noel had begun to realise that her future lay in a return to Dorset, although beyond that she had little idea what it was she was being called to do. She had learned enough to know that when you felt a call to a place, you had to trust that call, pick up your belongings and follow where it led you. Like Abraham, the key to it all was in trusting God. What she worked on together with Mary was a plan for the house she would leave behind in Chelsea. Together they would begin to convert it into a house for returning missionaries: those who, like Mary, had no place to go when they arrived in the unfamiliar capital of their home country; who, exhausted and disease-ridden, needed above all else a place where they could recuperate and renew themselves. Inspired by Noel's reasons for establishing her journal on her return from Asia, Mary asked that they might call it Life Line House, and long before Noel and Caroline left London for good, it bore that name.

DORSET

4

THE MOVE TO DORSET

So Abram went, as the Lord had told him.

Genesis 12:4

Stations fascinated Noel, particularly those in London. Their size and majesty made them places of portent before one even considered the nature of their purpose. They were full of energy, and as she walked into their great halls through the mist of steam, she came alive with the anticipation which filled them. Whenever she was bereft of ideas for *Life Line* she would walk across the bridge to Waterloo and stand and watch for a while. Mothers dragging unwilling children by the wrist, debonair men cutting a dash through streaming crowds, neat young women walking purposefully towards the platform. Everyone seemed to have a place to go to; the whole building was humming with movement and direction. Here people were being lifted out of their routine into a world which was removed in one way or another from the grey city life which they inhabited. There was no room for boredom or indecision. She would watch the few who didn't know the form with great pity, often moved to walk over and offer advice. The young family, the foreigner, the student; all were trapped in the speed of movement which threatened to trample their links with the future. But these were in a minority; the War had seen to it that most citizens understood the pattern of displacement and removal.

Once the day of her departure from London had arrived, she could not be entirely sure of her emotions. There was an elation which was not rational at the prospect of being on the move once more. After the sedate early years of her childhood, Donald had set in motion the thrill of the itinerant lifestyle by inviting her to the Far East, to work with him in Thailand, in the jungles. Together they had travelled around the area, never pitching their tent in one place for longer than a few months. The call to the Navy, when the War came to the Pacific, was a mere extension of a way of life. That Noel should be as involved as her husband was never questioned. Although the stay in London had been one of the most stable of her life, the city was the true home of the restless. The speed of life and the ferocity with which it was lived made it fit only for the adventurous and determined. Exhausting and debilitating as it had been, London had catered well for her agitated spirit.

But during this time she had learned how to pay heed to another part of her; a voice which could not be heard above the din of a crowded life without careful attention. It did not rest easy in the city and had drawn her to the country, again and again. It had been her guide and her solace as the pace and demands of London life became unbearable. Now, at last, it had led her back to her childhood haunts, to pack up her goods and begin a new life. The thrill was in the return to a nomadic existence; all the more now that she had cut herself off from her regular supply of income. It was also in the dream which Donald had given her with his extraordinary invitation to the Far East: the elation of rediscovering the vision and then following it, irrespective of the consequences. The content of the dream had never been specific, but she recognised the mood. It was a glorious sensation; to be reunited with the hope that is in you and to forge ahead with no more than the belief that you are being led by something greater than yourself.

Standing at Waterloo station with Caroline, surrounded by the last of their belongings, she took in the scene and won-dered if perhaps she were a little mad. The move to Dorset had made so much sense once the decision had finally been made. Over a year ago, her father had persuaded her

24

that he should buy a small plot of land which had become available, with planning permission, only a few hundred yards up the lane from her parents' house. She had viewed the field during one of her trips home and was delighted by the possibilities it held. Backed by an orchard, it had seemed utterly idyllic and she had accepted his offer. With a place to come to that allowed her some independence in Dorset, she visited more regularly; looking for some small dwelling which could be erected on the land. It had not taken her long to come across Giles Sidway, a local councillor who suggested that she purchase one or two of the old beach huts which had come up for sale as part of the council's new plans for tourism. The idea of having derelict beach huts as a country retreat appealed to her romantic nature and she snapped them up immediately.

And derelict they were. Two small huts with no more than a roof and walls, well made from sturdy wood, but weak from the constant battering of the elements and in terrible need of repair. With Caroline as audience and aide she had them transported the short distance to their new home and placed side by side. The process of conversion began. The two enthusiasts donned ancient overalls and workers' caps and attacked the old huts with paint. By the end of the summer holiday they had been transformed: with the first converted into a place for prayer, the large central room of the second was made comfortable with one or two old armchairs and a coffee table. Behind the divide they had installed a small gas cooker and covered the walls with shelves. A worktop allowed them to prepare simple meals and they had sewn curtains to cover the stacks of pots and pans. At the other end of the 'house' was an equal-sized room which now had two retired hospital beds against each wall and a beautiful oriental screen behind which they could change. It had served well as a holiday cottage and Noel had enjoyed adding to its effects with every visit, but as she now stood in the chill summer wind of an open station she wondered what had possessed her to believe that it would suffice as a home for her and her fast-growing child. Of course it could be considered positively luxurious when measured against some of the places she and Donald had lived in in the

Far East, but Caroline had only really known the relative comfort of Chelsea and was totally unused to the country. Was it cruel vanity to expect this dreamy child to cope with such a different way of life? She had made no plans to register Caroline in a local school and had no idea where the money was going to come from for their upkeep. Father Patrick had called it a sublime example of trust in God. At this very moment in time it struck her as the worst form of insanity.

As the train pulled alongside the platform in a cloud of steam she asked God that He give her some encouragement in this foolish pilgrimage on which she was about to embark. She needed a tangible sign that she was acting according to His wishes and not being led by her own desperation to escape. Caroline beamed at her, hoisting their worldly possessions under each arm and bounding toward the nearest carriage. The child was obviously caught up in the excitement of it all and saw it as the biggest adventure of her life. It had been sad to leave the school and to say goodbye to cherished teachers and friends, but she had never felt completely at home there and any opportunity legitimately to get out of school was welcomed. She clearly remembered the summer of two years ago: the freshness of the sea air and the clean smell of new paint, the creative possibilities which her mother had offered her and the chance to see their ideas come to life. It had been a magical time marred only by the lack of a companion with which to share it. The exhilaration of breaking up for the summer coupled with the memories of the last summer they had spent in Dorset was enough to keep her bubbling over with enthusiasm. But it was not enough to reassure her mother. The child was caught up in her new-found freedom. She could not see beyond the end of the holiday and had no concept of the uncertainties which lay ahead. Noel returned Caroline's broad smile, but she could not share it. They settled into an empty carriage and closed the door to muffle the scream of the whistle as it announced their departure.

The train had begun to pull out of the station and was gathering speed when Caroline leapt up and rushed to the window. A movement from the corner of her eye had caught her attention and as she stood she saw that it was the figure of a man pounding down the platform and trying to board the train. Noel turned the handle of the carriage door and watched as the weight of it crashed open. Leaning out of the train, she reached her hand to him and was almost pulled over by his weight as the man clutched at it and swung himself into the carriage. She fell back onto the floor as he steadied himself and pulled the heavy door firmly shut. As he regained his balance Noel looked up and recognised the sign she had asked for: it was Father David from the Friary at Hilfield, a long-time friend of her parents. 'Good Lord,' she said, 'am I pleased to see you!' And as he settled himself down for the long journey ahead she was able to talk to someone about the exodus which she and her child were embarking upon and the fears which lay ahead.

The two had not seen each other for so many years that there was indeed a lot to catch up on. He had followed her adventures in Siam with fascination and delight and had prayed for the young couple unceasingly when the war broke out. With the rest of the country he had heard very little about the precise nature of operations in the Far East, but had shared the pride of her parents when Noel's part in those operations became known. He had stood before God in his prayers on her behalf as she returned to England and empathised powerfully with the appalling position she found herself in after Donald's disappearance. But he had heard nothing about her spiritual pilgrimage in London, as she had not breathed a word of it to her parents. Now he was fascinated at the transformation as she talked quite freely about the will of God and His intentions for her. He would not have called her an ordinary woman but he marvelled at how the Lord works through each individual and misses no-one. She might not be ordinary, but she most certainly was not the first person who sprang to mind when considering spirituality. He remembered her as full of life and bursting with energy and sparkle; always ready for the next adventure, never about to say no to an exciting proposition. Full of courage (or naivety?) in the face of the unknown. But a woman hounded by God?

27

It was her earthiness, her normality which most pleased him. There was nothing pious or saintly about her, and yet the words which poured out of her were laden with a wisdom of which she seemed utterly unaware. He was amazed by these words coming from the mouth of such a 'worldly' woman. For surely Noel, of all people, was in the world? This bright, attractive woman who had been brought up in the world of cloth and fashion and who wore her clothes as if she were on the catwalks of Paris. One who had been unafraid to pull up her sleeves during the war and muddy her hands in the tainted world of the secret service. Noel, who had run with the rats of Fleet Street and never been trampled: who could talk the language of politicians like a man: who had the respect of all political parties in both the Commons and the Lords and had been asked to stand for Parliament. They said that nothing shocked her. After the life she had led, he was not surprised. What *had* surprised him was that the Lord should be talking to her so directly and apparently be preparing her for something very important.

As Noel talked of the pressure inside her head to get out of the maelstrom of London and of her growing disillusionment with things temporal she found in Father David a compelling listener. Watching her child's astonishment as she heard some of these ideas for the first time she confessed to the 'perfectly dotty' nature of their course of action and her complete inability to come up with a reasonable excuse for her behaviour. But the friar seemed delighted to give her exactly the kind of reassurance she most needed; talking of the noble path of waiting on the Lord's intention and the vital importance of the sacrifice which they were making. He spoke of discerning the will of God and of the central place of the daily office she was keeping. He also promised to put her in touch with Father Cox, a retired priest who had been working with the Franciscans for many years and who lived very close to her parents' home in Chideock. He would keep an eye on their situation and was most keen to hear about the direction which might eventually be worked out. Noel's countenance changed visibly during the course of their discussion and by the end of the journey she had the courage to tell him of her rather desperate plea that God give her some kind of a sign. He roared with laughter at that, and promised her that it was the first time, to his knowledge, that he had ever carried a message from the angels. Though as he helped her out of the carriage at Maiden Newton and wished her well, he wondered if she had even the slightest idea of how much of a revelation she had been for him that afternoon.

5

INTRODUCTION TO FAIRACRES

All shall be well and all shall be well and all manner of thing shall be well.

Julian of Norwich

The decision to leave London had been taken at the end of the summer term, seven years after they had first arrived. The end of an academic year had created a natural break and forced Noel to act on her growing disillusionment with city life. She had bought the beach huts almost two years ago and had been using them as a base whenever she could escape to the country. Now, as she recited her seven offices a day, she waited for the command which would allow her to begin this next stage of her life. What she was waiting for was some sense of purpose; some inkling of the importance of the beach huts, or the reason for a return to the country. What she had not expected was that the call to the country would come without any sense of direction once there. It was made all the more difficult by a well-timed host of invitations to stay. *The Times*, for whom she had been reviewing, offered her a permanent position. During her time as lobby correspondent, she had found herself in the extraordinary and probably unique position of being approached by all three parties and asked to stand for safe seats. When she refused the Conservative party on the grounds that she loathed public speaking, they had even sent her on a public speaking course to persuade her!

After the demise of *Life Line*[5] and years of struggling and battling for recognition, it seemed remarkable timing that she should feel the compelling urge to leave at the very time she was beginning to succeed. The incentives to stay were manifold, but the compulsion to leave was more powerful. Her final decision was taken blind, on the basis of an irrational need to leave the rat race and involve herself in something fundamentally spiritual.

With almost no idea of what she was going to do in Dorset, she spent the summer of 1952 with Caroline, making the beach huts fit to live in on a more permanent basis. In spite of a dearth of space, they decided to keep the chapel. It had the right feel to it. Light and airy with a window through which the sun poured, it was the sort of place which was immediately conducive to thought and prayer. It made a great difference to have a chapel in which to read the office.

The other priority was to establish the course of Caroline's education. It had always been a great ambition that she should gain a place at the Royal School, Bath; the school where Noel had been educated thirty years earlier. At eleven, Caroline had two years before she could sit the entrance examination. During their early years in London, Noel had made use of two boarding schools which accepted very young children. Now, with her daughter at home she could enjoy the opportunity of introducing her to the place where she herself had grown up. When Mary McCulloch mentioned the name of a friend who had recently retired from her position as headmistress, a new possibility presented itself. Within a matter of days the two women had met and agreed that Nora Greenwood would live with them and take Caroline for lessons during the next two years, to coach her for the Bath exam. In order to provide a basic income, Noel also agreed that she would work alongside her mother, weaving at the loom.

With the pressing question of Caroline's education sorted out, Noel began to relax into the Benedictine routine which had become her existence. As she moulded herself back into her childhood community she began to renew old acquaintances, with a new interest in those of the Church. She offered her services to the local paper and soon acquired a better understanding of life in Chideock and the surrounding area. It was not unusual for a woman to return to her parents, particularly when so many were aware of the tragic disappearance of Donald in the Japanese war. Very few had known of her emancipated existence in London, and so the change of pace and lack of direction were not a subject for discussion. For Noel, however, the change *was* extraordinary and had it not been for the discipline of her daily offices and the haven of the beach huts, she might have found the transition impossible. She had been used to living from one day to the next in London, but within the framework of *Life Line* she had always had a goal or a deadline towards which to work. Now, for the first time since the War, she had no idea what each day would bring and had no concept of how events were going to fit into the future. Father Patrick had taught her the rudiments of waiting on the Lord, and in every prayer she had asked that God might put her to His use and that the pattern of her life might be according to His will. In London it had been little more than a pious desire, so involved was she with the journal and with Fleet Street. Gradually, it had become a more profound force until the desire itself became the most important part of her life. Now, she was faced with the fact that although she still had little idea of the path which God had marked for her, there was very little other distraction to take her away from the central goal of discernment. The simplicity of the chapel and its restfulness was therefore a crucial part of her new life. In the early hours of each morning, in its stark wooden interior, she would sit in front of the wooden table, speaking the words of the office under her breath. After a prolonged period of silence, she would turn and open the door and fill her lungs with bright sea air.

It was a great help to her at this time that so many of her friends from London took up her offer of a stay in the country. These were the people whom she had met through her contact with Father Patrick or through the religious orders of which she had been part. Unlike her acquaintances in Fleet Street, they had both accepted and understood her flight to Dorset and their visits to Chideock provided her with necessary support and encouragement. Archimandrite Anthony, of the Orthodox Church, was one of the first to look her up, closely followed by Mary McCulloch on her way out to Africa once more. Each one joined her for prayer in the chapel, took long walks along the beach and through the woods, and talked until the small hours about her future and the possibilities which Dorset might afford. As she reflected on each visit when it was over, she noticed the thread which seemed to be running through her life, connecting everything she had done. The link to her life in London which these people offered allowed her to believe that her time spent there was not in vain but was somehow also a part of the same preparation as now. She had very little sense of what the future held, but she knew that when it became clear she would build on, rather than renounce, everything she had done.

Father David of Hilfield was true to his word and came to visit her new house on more than one occasion. They talked about the Friary and its life; and he took a particular interest in her rule of life as a Benedictine oblate. She told him about Father Patrick and the chance meeting which eventually led her to the convent at Malling. He knew of the Abbess Mary and listened to the stories about her with interest. It made sense to him that the two women should have understood each other so well and that Noel had been able to flourish under the Abbess' direction. Noel had an attraction to the community life and a feel for it which he had seen in few other lay people. He was impressed with her determination that the arduous seven office day be woven into the fabric of an everyday existence. After their meeting on the train he had wondered whether her calling was to challenge the clergy and religious with some new lay movement, and he put this to her now. Their discussion covered all the possibilities as they considered those whom Father David thought might help her. The woman who sprang to mind most vividly was Sister Mary Clare of the Order of the Sisters of the Love of God (SLG). He had known her when she was part of the Society of St Margaret in East Grinstead, and had been involved in the decision to move her to the SLG convent at Fairacres in Oxford. She had been there for just under ten years and had recently been nominated Mother Superior of that convent. Brought up in Oxford as Miss Sampson, her father was the Master of Brasenose College. For the twenty-five years she had been a contemplative nun she had been a force to be reckoned with; always combining the life of silence and contemplation with a passion for reading and learning. During her time at Fairacres she had campaigned for a more open approach to education, calling for ready access to books on the contemplative life and theology. She believed that while a contemplative order was necessarily enclosed, it did not have to be cut off from the world; for its true service was in praying *for* the world. So, she argued, the nuns had to have some sense of the Christian life *in* the world, that they could support it better with their prayers and intercessions. Using all the democratic means available to her she brought the need for change to the attention of those in authority and found a sympathetic attitude to her requests. The convent was going through a difficult time and Sister Mary Clare's energy and enthusiasm were seen as an opportunity to restore to Fairacres a sense of purpose and direction. Her appointment as Mother Superior was expected to bring radical change.

Armed with an introduction from Father David, Noel began a correspondence with the new Reverend Mother on the subject of the laity and their relationship to the religious orders. Mary Clare found in Noel an informed and perceptive ally, and it was not long before she issued an invitation to her to come to Fairacres so that they could spend some time together. At the time such an invitation was very rare: the Reverend Mother was not suggesting a formal retreat but an offer of hospitality. Noel leapt at the opportunity and travelled to Oxford.

Mother Mary Clare allowed her to stay in one of the small guesthouses, Fellowship House. She was also invited to attend chapel, though requested to sit behind the curtain which separated the nuns from the laity. She ate in her own room, away from the nuns' refectory. In later years Mary Clare was to abolish these practices of segregation and today the guests at Fairacres sit openly in the chapel and join the nuns in the refectory for meals. At this time, however, Noel saw no-one except

34

the Reverend Mother; but together they had a great many interviews and discussions. Young novices occasionally saw the two deep in conversation as they walked along the nut path at the end of the garden. This was extraordinary to them, as the tree-lined path was part of the enclosure and the novices had never seen any lay person enter this sacred garden.

The two women formed an instant and profound attachment. In their discussions they realised that they had each met someone who understood the same concerns and felt the same way about the spiritual life. Mary Clare was concerned that the contemplative Order be seen to be playing a crucial role in the life of the Church and recognised in Noel a woman who understood its importance. She was inspired that this intelligent and worldly laywoman should share her vision, and their time together was spent as much in discussion as it was in long periods of silent prayer. The Reverend Mother did not know exactly how her friendship with Noel was going to help her in the gradual renewal of the convent, but she felt sure that it would. On the other hand, Noel had found a kindred spirit with whom she could both pray and learn about prayer. She had never had such direct access to a contemplative order before and relished the chance to discover everything about it. Mary Clare was able to build on all her previous experiences of prayer and lead her to new ground. Everything she had felt in London and later learnt as an oblate was put into sharp relief by what she was learning at Fairacres. She too felt that their friendship was part of something much greater.

6

THE ORDER FOR LAITY AT CHIDEOCK

To thee, O Lord, I lift up my soul.
O my God, in thee I put my trust, let me not
be put to shame.

Psalms 25:1–2

For almost a year Noel's life consisted of little more than read-ing her office, making as many local contacts as she could and earning a living. During this time Nora became far more than a governess for Caroline. It transpired that she had been a Franciscan of the Third Order for years and she asked Noel if she could join her in the daily office in the chapel. She took a keen interest in the friendship with Mother Mary Clare and at the end of every visit to Oxford, Noel would come back and talk at length of what she had learned and about what she had been thinking. Nora was also at a turning point in her life and understood this search for the right way forward. The weight of both their prayers gave the need for clarity a renewed sense of urgency.

As it had always been for Noel, the decision to establish a lay order in Chideock did not come as a sudden revelation, but rather a creeping realisation that this might be the way for-ward. She and Nora had gone about their lives, weaving and teaching, saying the office at the chapel, and cultivating the acre of land around them to yield fruit and vegetables. Noel had become more and more convinced that this way of life could be shared by others among the laity; as a way of living in the world whilst keeping to the rule of a religious order. Her ongoing discussions with Mary Clare seemed to bear testimony to this: there was a great need among the laity for discipline and teaching, particularly on the subject of prayer. If they could develop a rule of life based on both the Benedictine and Franciscan rule, but adapted to their situation at Chideock, then they could open their doors to anyone who wanted to join them. The foundation of the Order would be contemplative prayer and the encouragement of the kind of approach to life which puts prayer above everything else. For, as Noel had found, if one has managed to achieve a discipline in prayer, an ordered place for God within each day, the rest of life seems to fall into step. After her discussions with Mary Clare, she also knew the importance of contemplative intercession; that is, standing before God on behalf of others. Of course, a lay order would never be an enclosed contemplative order and it was not her aim to compete with the vital role which these orders played in interceding for the Church; but a lay order would know the concerns of the day both nationally and locally and could be seen to serve some useful purpose in praying, not just for the Church but for the local community as well.

When this idea had finally surfaced and she had discussed it with all those whose opinions she valued, she agreed with Nora that the best plan would be to put their ideas down on paper. They would then be able to circulate a more definite suggestion to their friends who could add their own comments. They began to work out what this lay order would be like; its rule of life, its founding beliefs and its daily routine. With their joint knowledge of several religious orders they considered all possible angles: from the procedure for selection and membership to the accommodation required. When they had completed their first draft they sent it for comment to Mary Clare, Father David and the Abbess Mary. There was some criticism of an idea not well enough considered at its conceptual stage, and one or two searching questions to this effect. Mary Clare suggested that if Noel were to write a précis of the four Gospels in the light of the need for a lay order, she might gain a better understanding of the foundations on which the community would stand. This allowed Noel to think it through again and to feel certain of its purpose and aims. Overall, however, she was astonished to find broad sympathy for the idea and a great deal of warm encouragement from those people whose opinion she most valued. With a revised version of the planned order she now felt confident to take it a step further. So, she asked Father Cox formally if he would be prepared to continue with herself and Nora as part of a new community of the laity. As he had had to receive permission from the Bishop of Salisbury to take communion to the two women once a week, it was to the Bishop he now turned.

Bishop Key had been surprised when Father Cox had requested permission to take communion in a beach hut chapel and equally surprised to learn of two laywomen keeping so strictly to a rule of life. But he had been keen to keep an eye on the situation there and was pleased when the opportunity arose for further involvement with the developments in Chideock. He asked if he could see the plan which they had come up with and was impressed by its clear understanding of the community life of the religious. He was taken with the idea of the laity living in community and agreed that they might need something other than attachment to a monastery or mere pastoral involvement as parish workers. While he could not predict how successful such a venture would be, he was sure that it was an idea which should be given the chance to get off the ground.

With this in mind, the Bishop travelled to Chideock to meet Noel Wynyard and Nora Greenwood. Together, they took tea and talked at length about the proposed order. Noel explained her plans to build a larger house on the land which would, in the first instance, accommodate up to six members of the order. They talked through the rule of life and the plans for weaving, gardening, bee-keeping and work among the local community.

After this they spent some time together in the chapel. The Bishop found both women intelligent and articulate and was quite convinced by their dedication to this cause. He left having given them his blessing and requested that they inform him of future developments.

To have such backing was tremendous incentive to keep strictly to their combined rule. One of the dictums which they had agreed was that they 'get out of bed each morning as if it were on fire'. This characterised their new existence and they attacked each aspect of their lives with gusto. On the face of it, very little had changed: they still said the office seven times a day, Father Cox continued to come and say Mass in the chapel once a week, and they both wove and taught. Now, however, Noel was also taken up with the promotion of their community among the religious orders and the contacts she had built up locally. Her parents found the whole idea a little strange, but nevertheless agreed to recognise the plan. Noel had already concluded the enjoyable process of designing a new home on the plot of land her father had bought, as well as making all the arrangements for the architects and builders. Within a very short space of time the new house was ready for its first three inhabitants. The beach huts were not abandoned, however, and every morning the first prayers were said in the wooden chapel. The house was designed to accommodate six, but the hope was that once the order was established, individual cells could be built using the land next to the orchard.

There was tremendous excitement when the time came to move in. For the first time, Noel, Caroline and Nora were all under the same roof; there would be no more hectic inter-change between the Irwin family home and the beach huts. This new house had been created for the community and it meant that it was a most special building. It put in bricks what had previously only been on paper, and gave the whole venture more solid foundations. Perhaps, most importantly, it inspired in Noel a confidence which she had not always felt.

With the house in place and under the blessing of the Bishop all that was left to do was to wait for an interest from the laity. Noel advertised the venture in Malling, Hilfield and Fairacres in the hope that some of those who came regularly to those houses might get in contact. She was also in constant touch with her friends in London about the project, and they had promised to mention it to anyone they thought might be suitable. In the meantime, all she and Nora could do was to wait, to pray, and live their own lives as if already part of a community. This they did; following their own rule precisely and receiving communion. Noel was convinced that if this idea came from God, it would succeed. She had seen it happen so many times elsewhere; streams of people in need of help, rest, guidance, coming to the doors of a monastery or convent which never had to advertise its presence. If this venture was right, people would come to it of their own accord.

Yet no-one came and nothing happened. The two women prayed each day that they might be joined by others, but to no avail. They were devastated. Noel recalled her time as an aspirant in London, and was reminded of the fact that every time she seemed to take one step forwards, she was always knocked back again. Prayer became increasingly difficult as she fulminated against the God who had either wantonly mis-directed her, or allowed her to mistake her own desires for His, without correction. The house was expensive to keep and she was tired of making excuses every time one of her friends asked about the success of her new venture. She felt dejected.

Under such circumstances her response was to withdraw into herself, and she became more and more distant from Nora and Caroline. Pride would not allow her to communicate the full extent of her hurt and disappointment to those closest to her and her sense of isolation increased. She wanted the noise and distraction of London, and considered looking up her old contacts in Westminster and Fleet Street. On the day she had decided to do so, she was rescued by an invitation from Mary Clare to come and stay in Oxford.

Mary Clare was the sort of woman who could take one's rage without flinching. Somehow, she even seemed to permit it, in an environment characterised only by silence. Noel detailed her anger to the nun as if it were an inventory of life-giving supplies. From start to finish, she left out nothing. And Mary Clare listened.

After a week Noel returned to Dorset with new determi-nation and patience. The Reverend Mother had not only given the freedom to talk, she had put everything back within the framework of God. Together they had looked at the wreckage of Noel's aspirations and asked God to look, too. By refusing to leave God out of the conversation, Mary included the spiritual in the depths of her friend's despair and disillusionment. Gradually, Noel found herself able to offer God her pain, without any sense of irony.

She left Oxford with a book, lent from Mary's own collection. It was the writing of Father William Sirr, an Anglican priest who had established the order of *St Mary at the Cross* in Glasshampton. In the East End of London he had lived as a priest in a community known as the Society of the Divine Compassion (SDC), an early Anglican attempt at setting up a Franciscan community for men engaged with poverty and unemployment. He became their Superior for six years and stayed with them for more than fourteen. Over that time he felt he was being called to a life more of prayer than of social action. As there was no such contemplative order for men, he was released by the SDC to found one. In 1918 his new foundation began in an isolated and ruined stable in Glasshampton, Worcestershire. He remained there for eighteen years, keeping strictly to an austere rule of life which he had devised from his readings and experience. During this time he remained convinced that God was bringing into being a contemplative community of which he was the forerunner, although he was never to see that community come into being. For the whole of his life at Glasshampton not one man joined him for longer than a few months. His time there ended as it had begun; alone.

The experiences of William of Glasshampton gave Noel exactly the inspiration she was looking for. She read his works again and again, telling Caroline the story of the stone altar which he had so carefully built and asked the Bishop of London to consecrate. When the Bishop refused to come to Worcestershire, William had taken the altar apart, put the stones in a sack and travelled to London with them. It was that sort of conviction which Noel so admired. Father William may have remained a solitary at Glasshampton but where he was not joined by people, he was joined by their requests for inter-cessions. His dedication to prayer was recognised and so he prayed for them.

Noel returned to her chapel and began to do the same.

7

THE VILLAGE EVANGELISTS – CAMELFORD

'Lazarus, come out!'

John 11.43b

Six months later, Noel received a telegram summoning her to join a mission of the Village Evangelists in Camelford, Cornwall. Just before she left London, Father Patrick had suggested that she attend a lecture in the Sloane Square church, given by Brother Edward who believed it was his mission to tour the country and preach in every parish church. With a team of trusted friends and colleagues he spent two weeks in each parish, knocking on every door and encouraging people to come to one of the services they were organising. In London, Noel had been struck most of all by his extraordinary face and had talked with him after the lecture. In response to his query she had told him her Benedictine name, which he had passed on to Evelyn Gedge, the very impressive character who took charge of operations. Now, the Village Evangelists were moving toward Cornwall and wanted Noel to join them.

It was the sort of telegram that brooked no refusal. She read it several times, drew a deep breath and picked up the telephone. Carefully, she worded a response to be telegraphed back to Sister Gedge which made it clear that while she might be in the business of religion, mission was not her line. Privately, the very thought filled her with dread: it was something about stating one's faith baldly to the watching world in only a few words. Her faith had never been easily digestible. It was not something she could explain to herself, still less the man on the street. The rigorous discipline with which she structured her life made sense of a great deal of things that she could not explain, but she knew enough to understand that her daily office was not the sort of thing the average person could relate to. She had the utmost respect for Brother Edward and his mission, but her own faith in the Church was far from orthodox. She really did not think that she had it in her to stand on someone's doorstep and tell them that the answer to their problems was to return to church. If you cannot identify fully with the message, how can you possibly expect to be an effective advocate?

Noel had just satisfied herself with her argument for refusing, when she received a telephone call from Evelyn Gedge. 'We need you in Camelford, my dear. Come. No-one ever says no. I'm afraid we can't accept your refusal.'

Noel found herself in North Cornwall, two days later.

It helped that Camelford was a charming town and that the Anglican parish with which they were working was the sort of high church with which she felt comfortable. At the invitation of the parish priest, the mission had agreed to work in the village with the Methodists. A programme of services and open meetings had been planned and detailed on a print run of several hundred leaflets. The open meetings held in the Town Hall targeted those whose church attendance had lapsed, and were intended to be as informal as possible. There was always a key speaker who would give a testimony, and then the floor was open for questions, directed either at the speaker or the local clergy. Noel was encouraged by the number of laity among the Evangelists' team. In the past, Brother Edward had found that questions were more often about the Church and its lack of social involvement than of a theological nature; the meetings were usually as instructive for the priests as they were for the people who attended.

Having been met at the station, Noel was taken to the home of a woman who lived close to the parish church. There was very little time to make herself comfortable before she was

44

rushed over to the Town Hall for her first meeting. Here, she was handed a map with several streets marked out in red ink and told to call on every house in the street. Noticing how she blanched, Evelyn Gedge softened the blow by showing that all she need do was explain the Village Evangelists and leave a printed form with the list of meetings and services. If the occupants engaged her in conversation she should be up front about the mission but not frighten them off. One was permitted to accept a cup of tea as long as one covered all the houses in the time given. (Noel smiled at the military precision of the arrangements.) As she tried to digest the idea of engaging people in conversation about matters of faith, the real blow came. Not only must she go door to door during the day, she was expected both to attend every evening meeting and to take her turn in speaking at them.

As always, the anticipation of the event was far worse than the event itself. Right up until the knocker had made contact with the first door, she felt sure that she was not able to go through with this ludicrous scheme. Once the door opened, however, it was quite a simple matter to open the conversation with the young mother who stood there. She did not provide an enthusiastic reception but neither was she hostile. The few questions she asked prepared Noel for the next house, and so it went on. As the afternoon wore on, she got into her stride and caught herself beginning to enjoy it. At heart she had never left Fleet Street, and to be armed with a legitimate excuse to knock on people's doors, meet them, and even be taken into their homes, was a journalist's dream.

For the first night's meeting she could relax. As the newest member of the team it had been agreed that she should experience several house calls and evening meetings before she was asked to speak. So she settled into her chair at the back of the hall and listened to what people had to say. That first day there were very few people, but Evelyn had warned them that it was always so. What Noel was less inclined to believe were the figures which Evelyn had quoted for attendance by the end of the fortnight.

It was the journalist who listened intently to the grievances people had about the Church, but Noel's interest in the laity was also roused by the meeting. For the first time, she was hearing the voice of the true laity of the Church of England, state church that it was. And for the first time she was aware of a growing sense of pride in the work the mission was doing. If every citizen had the right to be baptised, married and buried in their parish church, then so too should they have the right to a free and frank exchange of views about that church. Tentatively at first, but soon with greater voice, the people talked about the fighting between the denominations and about the middle-class clique which was the church's congregation. They complained that services were never advertised and that the priests never called on them as they had in their parents' day. After two days, once the word had spread that these Evangelists were offering the chance to talk, the numbers at the meetings swelled and discussion turned to the education at the local church school and about wider education issues in Camelford. They told of the problems of bad housing and the lack of a community centre, and challenged the church to open itself up more to the community at large.

After such meetings it became easier to talk to people on their doorsteps. Noel was now armed with an understanding of the issues which were close to people's hearts. Once given the chance to talk about them, it seemed that the flood would never cease, and she found herself in an interesting situation: to avoid appearing too much like a social worker she had to root her conversation in Christianity. So it was, through her own decision, that she began to make reference to Jesus' ministry, retelling parables and stories of his healing and teaching. It was not hard to bring his social message into the conversation and her own reticence in this matter meant that she did it with some subtlety. After twenty minutes of chat, people would wave her goodbye with no sense of having been preached to. Yet somewhere along the line, they found that their attitudes had begun to change. It no longer seemed unrealistic to accept that a man who lived in first century Palestine could identify most strongly with the social needs of the community in Camelford. The next step was to show that the Church could do the same.

By the time Noel came to speak at the evening meeting, she had drawn great strength from her house visits and daily communion at the church. That said, nothing could convince her that speaking in public was anything less than an ordeal. Dredging up memories of the course the Tories had sent her on in London, she steeled her nerves and tried to calm herself. Clutching the sides of the lectern, she gave a talk about her life in London and the importance to her of St Mary's Church. She told them about the hectic pace of life and the need for silence and space in the presence of God. She explained how important the building and the liturgy had become; as a pool of tranquillity in her life, a place to rest and recuperate. It was in these terms that she spoke of communion: as something mystical and beautiful which drew you in and relieved you of the burdens which you carried. A time which was sacred, set apart from any other, which could energise and motivate you for the rest of the week. She acknowledged the vital nature of the mission (and this she now said with feeling) in getting the church and the community to talk to one another, and she begged people to take the next step and attend church. Only then could the church get to know them better and thus begin to address some of their grievances and needs.

By the time she had finished she was shaking all over and sank gratefully into the chair behind her. Having alerted the rest of the team to her fear of speaking in public, it had been agreed that Evelyn and the parish priest would be at the front with her in order to take questions immediately she had finished. In fact, a great many of the questions were aimed directly at her. It seemed that her story about the gradual discovery of a need for the space and silence of the church, as well as the realisation that to demand things of the church meant involvement, had been one with which people could identify. Their need for her to respond in person meant that she had no time to indulge in the terror she had felt; and on reflection she was grateful for this.

On her return to Chideock, two weeks later, she felt exhausted but pleased with herself. The intensity of visiting so

47

many people every day, of forcing herself to knock on another door when she wanted to crawl back to her guesthouse and hide, was draining. The physical trauma of having to stand up in the Hall and speak to increasingly large crowds never diminished. It had been brought home to her with force just how private a person she was. It is always strange to see yourself reflected clearly in a mirror held up to you by a new situation, and she was grateful for the journey home to consider her reactions to the mission at Camelford. Later, she would return to the town seven times and she became godmother and close friend to many of the inhabitants.

But now she was aware that she had kept her faith to herself for too long; fearful of its weak nature and of criticism. It was true that she could not articulate the sum of her beliefs with any degree of coherency, but she had drawn enormous strength from having to talk about it at all. Of course, her search for a spiritual director whom she could respect and admire had led her to discussion with many leading lights in the church, but in all cases she had been made more aware of her own inadequacies of training, not less. To date, the sum of her experience of God had come from the well of silence within herself which she had learnt to tap into. It had come from hours of contemplative prayer, from solitary walks through the countryside, from sitting on the cliffs and listening to the sea. She had engaged her brain in discussions with directors, and had learnt more about the retreat into silent prayer, but she had never learnt to be in the presence of God with and through another person. Even as a child she had learnt to rely on herself; and the pattern of her life thus far had confirmed that this was the case. It had taken several years in London to convince her that God too had not left her alone; and she now realised how much had changed since the days of returning from the Far East. There were few days now when she did not take it for granted that God was indeed there for her. Rarely did it cross her mind that she would not find Him each time she went to the chapel. She now realised, though, that the only time she had ever come across God through another person had been when she fled to Fairacres six months

48

previously. At Camelford she had talked with people she had never met, who had far less theological education than she. Yet it was here that she first realised the presence of God in those around her. Alone in the railway carriage, she opened the Gospel of Luke and started to read it with new eyes. Jesus had always seemed such a remote, mystical figure. An avatar, whose feet never quite connected with the muddy earth beneath. But here the physician Luke was talking about a man fully engaged with those around him, deeply involved with their lives. A man with a mother and siblings, with a stepfather and close friends. Every page she read gave her another example of God speaking through the wretched creatures He had put on earth; of truths revealed through the most ordinary and destitute. And suddenly she saw her work with the Village Evangelists as part of the unfolding plan. For over a year she had believed that God had shown her the future and that she knew what was in store. Her arrogance was her only mistake. The Order at Chideock had not been a wrong turning, it had simply not been the full picture.

HEALING

8

EARLY HEALING EXPERIENCES – EGGBUCKLAND

The Lord said to Abraham, 'Why does Sarah laugh...? Is anything too hard for the Lord?'
                                        Genesis 18.13a and 14a

Noel's return to Chideock was marked by a new spirit of openness and freedom. She seemed to take a more active interest in Caroline's work and talked with Nora for long hours about her experiences in Camelford. It struck her now that she had rarely shared as much as she should with her companion and she saw that she might have missed out as a result.

It didn't take long before she noticed that Nora was unable to share her enthusiasm for the Village Evangelists. Missions were not something Nora cared for; finding the confessionalism of it in rather poor taste. She was suspicious of this group of people who had commandeered Noel to Cornwall and felt unsettled by the change they had effected. The Order's lack of success had not had the same devastating effect on Nora, but she did not like to fail at anything. She had been hurt that Noel had gone to Fairacres rather than talk to her when it became obvious that the Order was not attracting people. It felt now as if Noel was prepared to talk because she had found new interest and motivation; but it was not something which Nora could feel part of. With Caroline's common entrance examination in sight, the Order represented the only plan she had for her own future. She disapproved of the missions and said as much; with the implicit warning that Noel's loyalties properly lay in Chideock.

The second invitation from the Village Evangelists was much less of a surprise. It came from a member of the Camelford team, who had his own parish in the Devonshire village of Eggbuckland. John Parkinson had been tremendously impressed with the way in which Noel had presented the Gospel and the mission; so unpretentious and unfussy. She had spoken straight to the heart of a great number of the parishioners and, he believed, had been instrumental in encouraging many of them back to church. His village had a tougher problem. There was a considerable suburb which had been created during the evacuations of the war. Set up as temporary accommodation, an increasing number of pre-fab homes now covered the hillside on the outskirts of the old village. The area had received no form of financial assistance to keep the houses in good condition, because it was widely hoped that their inhabitants would soon return to the east end of London. A decade after the War, the families were getting larger and their living quarters more and more dilapidated. They were cut off from the main part of the village both by their position and village prejudice.

The Reverend Parkinson felt the divide more strongly than many, and was anxious to try and close the gap. He had heard about Brother Edward from an old university friend who had witnessed a remarkable turn-around in his parish after a visit from the Village Evangelists. It was Evelyn Gedge's policy that priests who were interested in the missions should experience the work of the team in another part of the country. So, the Reverend Parkinson had been to Camelford and was all the more convinced that Eggbuckland needed Brother Edward's healing spirit.

Noel remembered the priest with some affection. He had been almost as nervous as she. They had talked together in the evenings when the house calls had been difficult and the meetings had not gone smoothly. She found in him a candid listener and enjoyed his sense of humour. Ringing him immediately the letter arrived, she asked what the dates were and whether

Evelyn Gedge had accepted Noel back onto the team. It wasn't until she was in the train that she remembered how the elation she had felt at the end of Camelford had been won at the expense of two weeks of anxiety and pain.

While the basic pattern of the Evangelists remained the same, the approach to the mission was different in each parish, with the local priest given free reign to target the most critical areas of need. The Reverend Parkinson spent the first evening detailing the cross-currents of the situation which the pre-fabs had created. He gave a full history of the evacuation plan and the response the village had made in the War. Having been there throughout, his perception of the turn of events was informed and well-judged and he passed this on to the team as essential background knowledge. A significant proportion of them would be working full-time among the pre-fabs, but the hardened attitudes were as much among those in the old village as elsewhere. It was there that the real difficulties would be. The ex-Londoners were tough, but they appreciated people who would talk back to them and weren't afraid to argue. The plan was to spend five days with the bulk of the team there, and then put in the concerted effort to include the rest of the village.

The leaflets with the times of services and meetings were always a useful entrée as one knocked on the door of a stranger. Noel loved the idea of trying to crack some really 'tough nuts' and would introduce the meetings as a forum 'to come and throw verbal stones at the priest and some other religious types'. She loved the plain speaking of these people and the lack of pretence; and like a chameleon she adapted herself. Her talks in the evenings were some of the most successful, and it was decided that she should be one of the team members who stayed among the pre-fabs for the whole two weeks. She made friends among them and was welcomed into their homes, often being asked to return. There was only one woman who remained deeply hostile throughout, heckling in the few meetings she did come to and slamming the door in Noel's face during house calls. Moira Clancy was renowned as the ringleader of a particularly unpleasant group and Noel was certain that if she could win her over, the greater part of the battle would have been won.

Knowing that she had no hope of a welcome at Moira's door, Noel adopted a policy of gentle deceit. At the end of one morning's work, she walked away from the site in full view of anyone who cared to be watching. As she became hidden by the brow of the hill, she took to the cover of the bushes, made herself as comfortable as possible and waited. It took about two hours before she saw Moira walk down the hill in front of her. She stretched her way out of her hiding place and fell into step behind her. After a few minutes the woman turned and stopped, deciding that it would be worth confronting Noel. She did so, letting off a stream of abuse and rhetoric which had been boiling away inside her for more than a week. Noel did not attempt to reply, but listened. Gradually Moira became calmer, and eventually fell silent. At this point Noel took her into the village, sat her down in a dark corner of the pub and asked Moira to tell her everything that she most loathed about the village and the church.

The day before the mission team was due to pack up and leave Eggbuckland, Noel was back at the pre-fabs inviting people to come to the final service in St Peter's. As she walked around the site she noticed that the door of a caravan which had never answered her calls was ajar. She knew from the others that the family who lived here were trying to cope with a terrible illness, but she had never had the chance to meet any of them. Now she felt bold enough to take up the opportunity which presented itself. As she knocked, the door swung open and she saw a young woman, resting on a sofa. Noel proffered a leaflet about the evening service and found herself asking if she could come in. It was not something she had done before. Within a very short space of time she found herself listening intensely to this articulate young woman who was dying of cancer. As a nurse, the woman was well aware of what was happening and how long she had left to live. She talked openly about her beloved husband, their two small children; and the pain of knowing she would be deserting them. Noel listened for an hour, feeling this woman's misery almost as if it were hers. Suddenly, without knowing what she meant by it, she said 'I think I can help you'. She asked the woman if she could pray with her and then promised to return the next day.

The final mission service that evening was eventful. The number of people who attended was more than the church could comfortably fit in and the 'east-enders' found themselves nestled against the old guard of Eggbuckland. The noise which they managed to create for the hymns was something wonderful to hear, and the prayers became a kind of free-for-all as the villagers joined in with the intercessions. Noel heard the name of the young woman mentioned and looked up to see Moira, pressed between two portly women, praying aloud for her friend. There was no doubt that something needed to be done and Noel resolved to see John at the end of the service.

Several hours later, the two were talking in depth at the rectory. Noel had recounted the peculiar nature of her meeting with the woman who had cancer; her impulse to enter the caravan which she had never done with any other house call, and her ridiculous statement that she believed she could help. Perhaps she had meant that by praying together the woman might find some new peace of mind? John was lost in thought. 'I think we may be talking about healing,' he finally said and began to explain what he meant.

During his training at Westcott house, between the Wars, John had been fascinated by the report spawned by the 1908 Lambeth Conference, *The Ministry of Healing*. It had led him to investigate the incipient healing movement, embodied by figures like Dorothy Kerin and James Hickson. As a curate he had sought out chances to hear these people and attend services given by them. He had joined the Guild of St Raphael[6] shortly after being ordained, and had determined to exercise his priestly gift of sacramental healing conferred on him by the Bishop. Since then, he had followed the debates in Synod with interest and reviewed every report that it produced with methodical care. Recently, he had begun advising the Bishop of Exeter on the experiences of the clergy in this field, for a new report to the next Lambeth Conference[7].

He explained all this to Noel, who had been utterly

ignorant of the whole healing movement. She quizzed him about the services he held, using the liturgy prepared by the Guild of St Raphael, the people who came to him and the effects of the services on their lives. Most of all, she wanted to know why she, a layperson, was becoming involved in this. As simply as possible, and trying not to alarm her, he outlined the difference between sacramental healing – which all priests may use by virtue of their ordination, and charismatic healing – which is a gift given to a few people. He did not dwell on this too long, but suggested that they hold a Guild service for the woman the next day, if Noel was in no hurry to return from the mission. She agreed, her mind still taken up with all the information about healing. John took her hand and said simply, 'Go back to the family and allow yourself to be open to what God may want to say to them. Let yourself be guided by the Holy Spirit and ask if they will come to a communion service tomorrow. Just the family, yourself, myself and a couple of the missioners. See what they say and we'll take it from there.'

To Noel's complete amazement, both the woman and her husband agreed to come to the communion service the next day. Transport would have to be arranged, as she was unable to walk. She was not a church attender, but had never lost touch with the faith of her childhood. Her illness had brought her closer to the dreams and hopes of her childhood as she watched her own children with new eyes. It was not faith which brought her to the church, but a sense of desperation that there was nothing more she could do for her children.

In the church, the scene could not have been more different to that of the previous evening. The small party of five did not sit on chairs but knelt at the altar rail, as John Parkinson went through the liturgy. Noel found it impossible to concentrate on the service. The familiar words of the Eucharist rolled over her: how could she be expected to lay hands on this woman? As she knelt at the altar, she suddenly saw that it was not a question of her doubts and fears. She was unimportant at this moment. Her role was simply that of the nuns at Fairacres, a contemplative intercessor. She was being asked to stand before God in the place of this woman and receive His grace for her. Now she knew that she had to cut out everything except prayer. Within a matter of seconds she was oblivious to the small group at the altar.

At the end of communion, John motioned to Noel to move behind the woman while he walked inside the rail, in front of her. As he prayed for her to be made whole, Noel placed her hands above the woman's head. For a few moments the church echoed with complete silence and then the woman reached out to her husband to help her up. In front of the small group, she stood up, turned and then rushed out of the church.

9

INTRODUCTION TO THE BISHOP AND HEALING IN GLEMSFORD

My days are swifter than a runner, they flee away.
                                                    Job 9:25a

Noel's own response to the healing service was one of complete terror. With as little fuss as possible she managed to leave Eggbuckland on the next train, slipping away from the church as John was caught in conversation with the two missioners. She knew that his next move would be to follow the young couple back to their home, but she wanted no part of that. So she fled.

The train journey was not long enough to settle her racing mind. She arrived back in Dorset and immediately took a detour to the sea, where she sat and watched and tried to take in the magnitude of what had just happened. On reflection, she realised, it would have helped to stay and talk with John. She really had no idea of what had happened, or how. She wanted to know if the woman was healed, what that meant, how it had occurred, what her own role had been. As the noise of this extraordinary event was silenced by the rhythm of the sea, she remembered the noise of her own emotions as the service began. At that point she had realised that it was not her, but God, who was in control of the situation. And so she now asked Him to take responsibility for her present confusion and distress.

Back at the house, she tried her best to slip back into the gentle routine. She spent long hours with Caroline, discussing her work and even taking over her Latin tutoring for a while. They chatted about the Royal School, whose common entrance was now imminent, and the normality of her own memories of the school were a great comfort to Noel. She walked to Silverbridge, her parents' home, and sat with her mother at the loom, knowing that she could find refuge in the complexity of the work and the shared silence which was the rule of the workshop. The times of prayer in the chapel became increasingly important to her in her attempt to keep a quiet mind and glean some sense of how this remarkable experience was to fit into her life.

Although she continued to find it difficult to talk to Nora, the lessons she had learnt at Camelford were tremendously important to her now. While her need for silence was the most pressing, she was at least aware of her need for people with whom to discuss this; and not necessarily a director or mentor. When John wrote to her at length, she gratefully began to correspond with him on the subject of healing, but it was when the young woman herself, Jane, wrote and asked if they might meet again that she felt she was moving in the right direction. With a brief warning that she had told no-one about the service in Devon, Noel replied to Jane with an invitation to come to Chideock and spend some time with them. Within a month, she did just that. Having left the family behind, she came to Dorset for a holiday and to find out more about the woman who had initiated such a dramatic change in her life.

For a week they took walks together by the sea and in the beech woods, shared a drink in numerous small pubs and enjoyed spirited conversation over dinner. Caroline was thrilled to meet her; she was so unlike any of the rather 'religious' group of friends her mother usually had to stay. Indeed, it had been a very long time since they had had any guests at all, and the chance of a new face at dinner was welcome. For both Jane and Noel the week was crucial to their understanding and digestion of the events which had taken place in Eggbuckland parish church. Each woman knew that their lives were about to be changed, but neither knew what that change would be. To be able to talk about it openly and honestly as well as praying together about it was a gift, and they each drew strength from the other. Just being with Jane answered some of the questions which Noel had; to see her walking and eating with new vigour. Jane's own testimony was to her renewed enthusiasm for life and her determination to begin again in some way. The doctors had not proclaimed a miracle and the cancer had not disappeared, but no-one who knew her was unimpressed by the reserves of energy which she had discovered and the light that now shone from her eyes. She had not been convinced of the need to become involved with the church, but was deeply touched by the prayer which she shared in Noel's chapel. Noel convinced her that the church was there for her and not the other way around, and Jane resolved to begin a small prayer group where she could continue to build on the strength she had found in Dorset. She also talked to Noel about the impact of the mission and her possible role in developing the good relations which had sprung up as a result. Noel found her an inspiration.

Being with Jane allowed her to dwell on the God-filled humanity of healing, rather than the human obsession with the power of the miraculous. She was the reason that Noel could focus on the simplicity and normality of the healing spirit of God, the sense that this was the way in which life had been originally ordered; whole and fulfilled. Restoring that wholeness was therefore the 'norm' rather than something extraordinary. Her thoughts were directed away from the questions of a complete cure and towards what Jane could do *now* in her life and for others. And she began to realise that not only can you see and come to God more easily through His creatures, but that it is through these creatures that God wishes to rebuild the perfect creation that was His. If wholeness is the proper pattern of things, then people can be made whole in order to continue that process. As they read the Gospels together in the chapel, she identified these ideas with the building of the Kingdom of God of which Jesus had so often talked. Healing was simply the restoration of a broken

62

vessel to its original form, with a view to it being of some use once more. Jane knew this without having to articulate it; and had sought out Noel so that she might learn what use she could now put herself to. But what was Noel's part to be?

After Jane's return to Devon, Noel tried to broach the subject of healing with both Nora and Father Cox. The former's response was one of simple disbelief. It was not something she had ever come across, and as a practical person she preferred logical or rational explanations. She believed it to be a dangerous occupation, undertaken by people with an inadequate grasp of its dangers and complexities. She was not interested in Noel's own experiences and did not press her further. For her part Noel said no more, not wishing to antagonise her. Father Cox, however, was more gentle. He suggested that he might contact the Bishop about it and see what he said. Already aware that there was a wide variety of approaches to and beliefs about healing, Noel was sceptical, but Father Cox knew that this was something which the new Bishop, William Anderson, was particularly interested in. The Bishop had already received positive reports about Noel from his predecessor, and would be interested to hear of Noel's experiences with the Village Evangelists. Paul Cox knew that there were those who possessed the charismatic gift of healing and believed, with Bishop Anderson, that it was of the utmost importance that the Church recognise such people officially, so that they remain within the Church. It was not easy: healing was still considered a fringe occupation and something to be wary of. He wondered how the transition had been made from a vibrant young Church in the first century, for whom the healing of the sick was a central concern, to the inert formal structures of the institution which it had become today; a Church where the presence of God's spirit was something to be investigated at official level and then hidden under the carpet. Father Cox had always believed that the true spirit of the Church could never be quenched, and that it was what had kept the Church alive throughout the centuries; but he also knew that this spirit was more often to be found in the laity than among the hierarchy. It was at grass roots level that the Church was alive, in the

63

least expected places. It was the spirit which led: the Church merely had the occasional insight to keep up with it.

Father Cox asked to meet Bishop Anderson to discuss Noel Wynyard with him. Sitting in the South Canonry of the Cathedral Close, he told him in some detail of the lay Order in Chideock and its lack of success. More than anything though, he talked of Noel herself and of her story. He emphasised her normality and its uneasy coexistence with her openness to God. Finally he told the story of Jane and of John Parkinson's intuitions about Noel. Bishop Anderson listened with interest. It sounded possible that this woman had indeed been blessed with the gift of healing. He considered whether the Devon experience was enough to go on, and decided he would call her to Salisbury to meet her.

At the same time as Noel received Bishop Anderson's letter, Evelyn Gedge telegrammed her with the summons to another village mission. The dates on both were the same and she found herself in a dilemma. After talking with Evelyn, it was agreed that she could miss the period of preparation which normally preceded the missions, joining the group on the day that the mission was to be launched. This time she was to travel to Suffolk, to Ray Walls's rural parish of Glemsford. He had been the 'priest missioner' at Eggbuckland and one of the two who had taken part in the service for Jane. Although they had not been in touch, she knew that he was sympathetic to the concept of healing, and so wrote at some length about the way things were moving and Bishop Anderson's request to meet her. Ray Walls was sorry they would not have her as part of the preparation for the mission but was grateful for what time she could put in. He was most interested in the fact that Bishop Anderson might recognise her as possessing a charismatic gift of healing and agreed with her that such a gift was indeed a frightening thing. His own warning was that each 'patient' should be properly prepared and spiritually ready for the healing service, and he spoke of the need to spend time with them, both before and after the service. Noel was grateful for his advice and as she prayed that she might discern a little more of God's plan for her in Glemsford, she thanked Him that she would be working alongside a man who understood and could guide her.

Bishop Anderson talked with Noel in his study for an hour about healing. With so little effort, her involvement in this area of God's work seemed to be gathering pace. It seemed extraordinary to her that only a few weeks before she had not even known it existed. Yet each new encounter seemed to explain more to her and helped her to build up a clearer picture of the healing ministry. The Bishop spoke of the need for discernment (which would no doubt be increased with her visit to Suffolk), of official recognition by the Church if indeed she had a gift, and then of training so that it might be properly put to use. Leaving for Glemsford two days later, she received a letter from a Father Hopkinson in Wareham. After the mission, he requested that she get in touch with him. The Bishop had suggested that he might be the person to teach Noel a little more about the history of healing and its place in the church.

10

THE END OF THE ORDER AND TRAINING

Lord, thou hast been our dwelling place in all generations.
Psalms 90:1

At Glemsford, Noel was part of a healing service for a young girl incapacitated with a skin disease. The process of her recovery had begun almost immediately afterwards, and by the end of the fortnight she was able to take on some light work on the farm where she lived. Ray Walls documented the service and Noel's part in it, and sent his account to Bishop Anderson. It seemed to him that their experiences in Suffolk were confirmation of what the Bishop suspected, and he was keen that Noel's gift be recognised and used by the Salisbury diocese.

Though less shocked by the events at Glemsford, it was only the human experience of Jane's visit which allowed Noel to take it all in her stride and continue as part of the mission. The fact that it had occurred so near to the beginning of her time there also meant that she had the advantage of time with Ray, to talk through what had happened. True to his own beliefs, he and Noel had spent a significant amount of time with the girl at the farm to prepare her for the service held in her room. Thereafter, Ray took Noel on his visits to the farm, to give her some idea of the kind of follow-up which he believed necessary. This allowed her to place the healing within the wider framework of an ordinary life, lived each day in the light of its new wholeness. It also helped her to digest what had happened.

The first thing Noel did on her return was to telephone Father Hopkinson and arrange a date to visit him. The drive from Chideock to Wareham is one of the most beautiful in Britain and Noel enjoyed it in her red open-topped sports car in glorious early summer sunshine. Father Hopkinson was by now an old man, and had retired from his official position in the church to be an unofficial 'assistant curate'. During his lifetime, however, he had written one of the most frequently used books on pastoral theology[8] and the Church continued to make frequent use of him. He was extraordinarily well-read and an expert teacher; as well as being an experienced spiritual director. He had been concerned with the question of healing in the Church since he was an ordinand, and had been one of the founding members of the Guild of St Raphael. With her minimal knowledge of Church matters, Noel was unaware of his experience as she stepped inside his home for the first time. As such she was unaffected and unembarrassed in his company, answering his questions freely and speaking of her experiences with frank honesty. He took to her immediately and, after explaining what the Bishop had in mind, was happy to suggest an extensive 'training' period: wanting her to read all those books he believed to be the 'classics', as background to a subject about which she knew so little. It would also involve a slight reorientation of her prayers. He was delighted to discover her connections with the Fairacres convent and suggested that she talk long and hard to Mary Clare about her new direction and the relationship between prayer and healing. While he would train her to think about this controversial subject and to be able to answer any question raised by sceptical priests and laity, Mary Clare was the best person to be equipping her for the spiritual journey ahead. It was up to Noel to decide how best to reconcile the plans for the lay Order with this new direction. He would meet her again when she had a clearer idea of what she wanted to do.

It was something which Noel had been putting off for some time. Caroline had taken the common entrance exam two months ago and was now simply biding her time with Nora. There continued to be no word of interest in the 'lay Order', although the two women still lived strictly according to their rule. Since the start of her involvement with the Village Evangelists six months ago, Noel had been travelling regularly and had seen very little of Nora. Their friendship had been reduced to formality by their disagreements about mission and healing, and Noel realised that she had not spoken to Nora about the future at all. Now, in June, with the end of the summer term in view, she knew that the time had come to talk frankly about the Order and where they were both going from here.

When Noel and Nora finally did sit down together to talk, it came as a great relief. They refrained from discussing the details of the past six months, and if there were any grievances they kept them to themselves. What they did discuss, however, was the Order and its failure. Neither had ever really faced the truth of this and to do so now eased the burden. They talked about what had gone wrong, whether there was anything more they could have done and how important it had been for each of them. Noel spoke about how she believed it to have been an important step on the road to their respective futures, but that it had never been the whole future for either of them. Nora listened as Noel outlined where she thought it might be taking her from here, and wondered if she would ever have such a strong sense of direction. She had been considering her future for some time now and had decided to respond to a sick friend who needed her help. As deputy head of her previous school, the two had been close companions. She had retired with a debilitating illness, and had been begging Nora to come and look after her. Now it seemed that that was the path she would take.

They spent a long time discussing the Order and how they would 'fold' it. Noel agreed to contact all the religious houses and let them know that it was no longer a going concern. She had already talked with Father Cox who had offered to continue to bring communion once a week if it was still wanted. Both women loved the rule of life they had worked out and decided that they would take it with them and keep to it, separately. It was an important link between them and their earliest dreams for the community, allowing them to leave one another on a positive note.

When confirmation came through that Caroline had passed her entrance exam Noel wrote to Father Hopkinson to let him know how things were working out. The lay Order would be officially closed in July, although she and Nora would continue to keep to the rule of life they had devised. Noel enclosed a copy of the rule so that the priest could see what her discipline consisted of and could comment, if he felt comment were required. She also explained that with Caroline's departure to boarding school in September, she would be spending the summer with her daughter. Thereafter, she was free to dedicate herself full-time to his training. At this time she also wrote a long letter to Mary Clare, to explain what had happened since they had last met. She was mindful of Father Hopkinson's advice that she could have no better guide on the subject of contemplative prayer and was eager to know Mary Clare's thoughts on this new direction. Mary's response was measured. She had always believed in the idea of the lay Order and had felt that Noel was pioneering something tremendously important. However, she could not argue with the fact that it had fallen flat and so agreed that this might be a new direction. She was not against the idea of healing, although she knew very little about it. She suggested that once Father Hopkinson had agreed a 'timetable' for his training, they could arrange another visit to Oxford and they could talk about her future.

After a wonderful summer holiday and a painful separation from her daughter, Noel was ready to accept whatever time-table Father Hopkinson thought necessary. She had received a letter from the Bishop which suggested that, on the basis of correspondence he had had with the Reverend Parkinson and the Reverend Walls, she undertake extensive training with Father Hopkinson. If she was able and willing to do this, then there was the possibility that Bishop Anderson would commission Noel as a healer for the Diocese of Salisbury. Quite what such a job entailed or whether she was the person to do it, would be left to the discretion of Father Hopkinson.

The gift of healing is not enough to equip one for the work

of healing. That much had been proven to Noel at Eggbuckland. It needs to be channelled and understood, first and foremost by the person who has been blessed with it. It had been a frightening enough experience but at least her obedience to a disciplined religious life had given her the framework within which to comprehend it. The first lesson she would learn was that healing was misunderstood by the majority of people: the Church not least. There was a great deal of prejudice to be confronted, and assuming that ignorance was the root of such prejudice, the best antidote was knowledge. If she had the gift, then the knowledge which comes through experience would follow in due course. What she needed, above all, was a thorough grounding in the history and science of healing. To combine such an academic training with a disciplined prayer life would be the best form of preparation she could have; and Father Hopkinson was anxious that she should be well-trained. He had seen too many charismatic healers sidelined by the Church for their inability to defend themselves with an orthodox theology. He believed passionately that the resurgence of healing which seemed to be taking place this century, was the work of the Spirit. The Church could not afford to ignore it. It was a spirit which breathed life and reconciliation into a dying and broken institution. But too many centuries of marginalising this spirit had left the Church with no theological tools to handle the phenomenon. And with an energy as explosive as this spirit promised, Father Hopkinson knew that the Church had to learn how to cope with it. Those with the gift of healing are not confined to the Church; nor were they in Jesus' time. Such people have access to a power which can bring wholeness and health to people at the most vulnerable time of their lives. It is, however, a gift which seems to be given regardless of a person's ability to manage it, and Father Hopkinson had been scarred by one too many human errors in this supernatural arena. Evidence of scores of laity who could heal was a gift of God to His Church, at a time of desperate need. But it was also a test. And to pass a test set by God, one needs to have more than a little mettle and spiritual discipline.

70

Noel's first task was to read the complete works of Bishop Gore in an attempt to give her the background to the sort of questions which she might be asked both by the sick and their priests. A commissioned healer would travel throughout the diocese and take healing services for those who wanted them. In most cases the healer would lead the clergy, although Noel would never be permitted to hold a service without the parish priest. If the priest was deeply sceptical about healing, it would be her job to persuade him otherwise. If she was unable to do so, the service could not take place. That was motivation enough for Noel to learn as much as she could.

Although she had never enjoyed public speaking, she enjoyed facing people who disagreed with her, and trying to convince them of the truth as she saw it. One of the high points of the missions had been her discussions with Moira. The more she read, the more she enjoyed her conversations with Father Hopkinson, as he played devil's advocate. She had received very little formal education, but her twice weekly sessions in Wareham were as exciting as tutorials at university. She took her study very seriously.

When not travelling to Wareham, she spent much of her time in correspondence with Mother Mary Clare at Fairacres. They had begun to develop their understanding of lay involvement with contemplative prayer; and now saw that it might have a very important part to play in the healing ministry. If indeed it were the case that the majority of those with the charismatic gift of healing were laity, then it was essential that their ministry was rooted in the same kind of discipline which a priest's life necessarily had. The rule of life which Noel had devised was actually more important now than it been last year; providing the foundations upon which a strong ministry might be built. Mary Clare spent many hours in silent prayer with her friend, as they placed before God her gift and her training. She also taught Noel more about contemplative intercession: something which would become crucially important as she was inundated with requests for healing. For Mary was certain that this would be the case. William of Glasshampton[9] had received more requests for prayer than he had been able to cope with; the nuns at Fairacres knew about such a flood of requests. It was a fundamental need in society which was not being addressed by the whole of the Church. Thus, those few who were seen as 'professionals' in the art of mending the human relationship with God, became exhausted by the demands on their time and energy. It would be the same for Noel. Perhaps worse, for she would be expected to travel to those who needed her. As such, Mary Clare felt it was her duty to prepare her with the spiritual discipline needed to preserve herself in the face of others' pain.

11

THE COMMISSIONING

And he called the twelve together and gave them power and authority over all demons and to cure diseases, and he sent them out to preach the kingdom and to heal.

Luke 9:1–2

Noel underwent the rigorous process of training with her two directors for more than three years. Twice a week she drove to Wareham in her red spitfire, for debate, instruction and advice. Twice a month she travelled to Faircares for a few days of silence with the Mother Superior. During this time her life began to take shape. She re-met an old army colleague of Donald's from Burma, now based in Devon. He travelled to see her regularly and, at an otherwise lonely time of her life, she enjoyed the companionship he offered. From their first reunion he had been suggesting marriage, but it took some thought before she could accept him. Father Hopkinson had been dismayed: he saw Noel's life in the future as a crusade. The fact that she had a daughter had not seemed to interfere with this too much now that Caroline was at school. However, the introduction of Major James Heath into the picture warned more of a family unit. None of the great women in the Church had managed to achieve their goals with a family in the background; it simply wasn't done. There were some sacrifices that had to be made, as a pioneer. Noel disagreed. Her training with Father Hopkinson and Mother Mary Clare had confirmed that her life's calling was to the ministry of healing. She did not know what this yet meant in practical terms, but knowing

73

what God's purpose for her was had given her a deep contentment. She would not jeopardise that by cutting corners or falling short of His expectations for her; but in a profession which was concerned exclusively with the restoration of wholeness to a person's life, she knew that the chance to restore her small broken family was not to be passed up. If, in the process, that meant redefining the role of the woman in that family, then so be it. Before saying yes, she tried to be certain that James knew what he was offering to take on. They were married at Wootton Fitzpaine church in the summer of 1955.

These years of training for Noel were part of a much broader plan envisaged by the Right Reverend William Anderson, Bishop of Salisbury (1949–1963). He saw the revival of the healing ministry, initiated by Dr Percy Dearmer and James Hickson, as being of as much importance as the eruption of missionary zeal of the seventeenth century. He felt that the Church was witnessing the beginning of something quite extraordinary and he wanted 'to take part in this great spiritual revival, which is one of the glories of this tempestuous century'.[10]

He had brought in Arthur Hopkinson as his deputy in what he freely referred to as an 'experiment': 'the attempt to make (Divine healing) a normal part of the Church's work and not a mere extra'.[11]

His belief was that healing should be an 'integral part of the pastoral work of every parish priest', but he realised that for this there was still a great deal of preparation which needed to be done. Knowing that it would take many years before the necessary training of priests could be put in place, Bishop Anderson had decided to follow the example of the Diocese of Manchester. There, the Bishop had used the charismatic gift of a member of the laity, Helen Noble, to illustrate the crucial importance of this ministry for the Church. By commissioning a member of the laity (in itself an unusual move), the clergy were being forced to think again about the responsibility for healing which their ordination had placed on them. Unlike the Bishop of Manchester, however, William Anderson would authorise Noel to exercise her charismatic gift in any parish to

74

which she was invited by the parish priest. She would not be based in one church, as was Helen Noble, but would be an itinerant. If his intuition was correct, she would be called to move throughout the length and breadth of the diocese, at the invitation of those who needed her. The simple act of identifying the need would be enough to convince some, while the extent of her travelling would provide tremendous publicity for this revival. He was convinced that she was an integral part of God's plan. Her measured manner, her breeding, and her attractive appearance were enough to coax the most determined opponent. He was in no doubt of the extraordinary nature of her gifts, but it was her ordinariness which he valued most. She was magnetic but not hypnotic, intelligent but not boorish. And with the foundations of Father Hopkinson's training to sustain her, he was quite sure she was the advocate for whom he had prayed.

Noel remained unaware of the extent of this great man's hopes for her. While she had become a close friend of Father Hopkinson and his family, she had spent very little time in the company of Bishop Anderson. Nor had she discussed the detail of his plans for her. Thus, a month after her marriage, the Bishop called her to Salisbury to explain his vision. At the end of three years of preparation she was encouraged by the way in which this fuller perspective completed her training. She understood how she fitted into the wider picture and was touched by the Bishop's enthusiasm and faith in his experiment. Two weeks later she returned to the South Canonry and was taken into the chapel. In a simple service, the Right Reverend William Anderson commissioned Noel Heath officially to heal the sick in his diocese.

Immediately after this Noel joined the Guild of St Raphael, at the advice of Arthur Hopkinson. The great advantage of this was that she had their small book, with its printed service, permanently to hand. It was tangible and sane; qualities which would recommend it greatly to both the cynics and the fearful. And it was fear that was the greater part of the hostility which she expected to meet. Her first job in Devizes baptised her into the ecclesial scepticism which was to characterise her

75

ministry for years to come. Having been asked by a parishioner to engage Noel Heath's gift, the rural dean called her to his home and grilled her on the subject of healing. She left several hours later battered but elated, and rang her director from the nearest telephone box to thank him for his preparation. Almost immediately the rural dean recalled her to a hastily convened gathering of all the priests in his deanery.

The spiritual revival of the healing movement had begun at a grass roots level, rather than as an institutional initiative. It was influenced less by the clergy than the missionary movement of two centuries ago had been. Individuals like James Moore Hickson had rocked the Church, not so much with the evidence of their gifts as with the need which their ministry had identified among the laity. Everywhere Hickson travelled, he was greeted by crowds of thousands. Many were seriously disabled by their illnesses, but they came to be in the presence of the healing spirit so that they might be renewed. In some way, each one left healed: either in body or in spirit. Hickson was a powerful personality, but when people recalled the day they were drawn to his meetings, it was the power of the spirit that made the greatest impact. The challenge Hickson offered the Church was to harness this gift and use it at a time when Church attendance was falling fast. As a lay person, he challenged the Church to make use of its un-ordained majority; to recognise the energy and vigour which their inclusion offered and not to be afraid of it. As his voice was joined by those of Helen Noble, Janet Lacey[12] and Dorothy Kerin in Britain, Theresa Neumann in Germany, and Agnes Sandford and Kathryn Kuhlman in America, the Church was increasingly challenged both by the ecumenical nature of the healing ministry and the unmistakable lead which it gave to women. Within the Church, the few who had taken this phenomenon seriously had tried to systematise it into a sacramental theology[13].

William Anderson was well aware of this background and understood the part which he was calling Noel to play in it. He was not afraid to give authority to the laity, nor indeed to women. What he was concerned about was that those to whom

76

the Church gave such authority were as well-trained as any member of the clergy. With Arthur Hopkinson, he believed that the experience of the healing ministry in the first half of the twentieth century offered two methods of divine healing. The theologians emphasised the sacramental nature of the work, while those endowed with the charismatic gift (Hopkinson referred people to the special *charisma* bestowed on individuals of which St Paul writes in 1 Corinthians 12:28–31) were led by the Spirit. As accredited ministers of the Church, priests were sanctioned to use the sacramental act of the Laying on of Hands. As individuals with the gift of healing, James Hickson, Helen Noble and others all used this same outward sign. In his diocese, William Anderson wanted to make it plain that there was no rivalry between the sacramental and the charismatic. This was his response to the lead which the laity had given in the Healing Ministry. Noel had been as well-trained as any priest, but she was commissioned to work solely alongside the parish priest and would use a liturgy which had been used almost exclusively thus far by the clergy. By acting only in co-operation with the priest, asking him to join in both the laying on of hands and the prayers, the Bishop hoped that he had found a way to combine both aspects of healing. He did not know where it would lead, but he trusted that the dynamic of this world-wide movement was the initiative of God. As such, he had faith that his experiment would succeed.

Noel had not shared his certainty. From the start she laboured under the delusion that no-one would come to her. Aware of the opposition of the clergy, she felt sure that they would block those who needed her. Three years ago she had taken refuge in the knowledge that she would never work alone, but with the confidence her training had given her she now wondered whether close co-operation with the clergy was such a wise decision. On the other hand, she had seen her plans for a lay order collapse for want of interest and she knew that she had to have the support of the Church. Yet it was her experiences with the lay order which were now uppermost in her mind. She was not sure that she had the strength to cope with another failed initiative.

77

The only publicity she received was an article written for the *Sarum Gazette* by Arthur Hopkinson[14]. The Bishop had asked him to explain the history of the present healing revival and the part which the diocese of Salisbury hoped to play in it. The article was widely circulated and reprinted several times. Within days of being published, the telephone calls began to flood in. In direct contrast to the Order she had tried to establish, she no longer had problems with people coming to her. Each week she drove hundreds of miles to take part in services throughout the vast diocese. At first she worked only in churches, but as the need arose she took part in bedside services. These were begun in private homes, but as her reputation grew, she was invited into the hospitals to work alongside the chaplains. To avoid charges of being 'an itinerant magician'[15], she accepted two decrees of discipline. Although she could debate the importance of healing at length with the priests, it was always to be done in private. She would not address public meetings. It was important to her that her work was kept purely personal, one-to-one. As Hopkinson put it, 'Healing, not talking about healing, is her job. It takes the whole of her time.' The second was that she should not work outside the diocese. There were two reasons for this: firstly because 'a wandering ministry often means that the healer works promiscuously, having little part in the proper preparation of the patient, or in following up the case afterwards'. The second became apparent very quickly: work within the diocese would keep her as busy as she could be. Each case was carefully recorded and sent to the Bishop, which doubled her workload. Despite the full-time nature of her job, she received no payment from the Church, so unorthodox a venture was it. This did not worry her unduly. Healing was an affirmation of the spirit; and this was as true for her as it was for those she was called to. However, with no independent means to support her, she knew she would have to find some method of financing herself. The knowledge she had gained from building her house in Chideock provided the inspiration she was looking for. The majority of her life with James would be spent moving from one house to the next as they exploited

78

the boom in the property market, so that the project might continue.

In 1963, Bishop Anderson was succeeded by a man for whom the healing ministry was not a priority. At the same time, Arthur Hopkinson died. It was not the intention of either of these great visionaries to leave Noel in a void, however. Only two years earlier a difficult case had introduced her to Father Gilbert Shaw, and the Bishop had recommended that he accept her for spiritual direction of a more advanced kind.

12

THE TRANSITION – GILBERT SHAW

I will show you, hear me; and what I have seen I will declare;
What wise men have told and their fathers have not hidden:
Job 15:17–18

Noel was quite certain that it was the movement of the spirit that had brought her to Gilbert Shaw. The work that she was being called to do quickly became more intense and varied; she spent the whole week travelling around the diocese and each day was full from morning to evening. She still made time to visit Mary Clare for prayer and the chance to talk things through, but the scale and complexity of her work was taking her further away from her original mentor, Father Hopkinson. While he had trained her in the rudiments of theology and pastoral work, he had always seen his role as that of the teacher. Once she had learned all he had to teach, she would be ready to start the real learning. He hoped he could equip her for most things, but he knew that her experience in the field would quickly outstrip his. Thus she turned to Mary Clare for emotional and spiritual support. At Fairacres, she could revive herself and pray, uninterrupted by the telephone. But Mary Clare knew very little of the healing ministry itself. She gave Noel the time to talk and was always interested in what she had to say, but Noel yearned to speak to one who *knew*.

The most difficult thing for Noel to cope with was the exhaustion which accompanied her new life. As Father

Hopkinson had predicted, it was difficult to juggle a home life with this ministry: James had been told exactly what would be expected of Noel, but neither of them had ever believed that the demand for her work would be so great. He complained rarely and adapted to her long hours with very little fuss. But he still expected her to return every day and he did not consider it unreasonable that she should continue with the normal household duties whenever she was home. With her child at school, these were less than they might have been, but Noel still battled against the inequality of the situation. She found it impossible to explain to him the degree to which healing sapped her energy, nor the reason why she found herself taking on board so many of her patients' symptoms. When she came across the case of a ruthlessly disruptive child of eleven, she felt ready to give up. She knew that she had met her match and nothing she could say, do, or pray for would combat the situation. She returned to Chideock and rang the Bishop for advice. Without giving away her own hopelessness, she asked him if he was familiar with anyone who dealt with exorcisms. He was silent. Then, carefully, he asked about the details of the case. Committed to healing as he was, his sceptical mind was loath to jump to the supernatural conclusions to which the evidence pointed. He talked the case through with Noel to satisfy himself that she had considered all possible angles. Finally, he persuaded her that she should enlist the help of both Fairacres and Hilfield in praying with her.

Feeling bereft of support, Noel rang her friend, Iulia de Beausobre, in London. The women had been introduced to one another by Archimandrite Anthony of the Orthodox Church. Iulia had survived several years in a concentration camp during the War and had somehow found the strength to write about it on her release. Her books were shot through with her powerful belief in Russian spirituality and showed just how much she had relied on the stories of the saints to keep her alive. Noel had always found a home in the Orthodox Church for her beliefs in the supernatural. In their writings and teachings they took seriously the realm of things not understood, and were not as obsessed as the western churches had become by the need to square their theology with eighteenth-century rationalism. She came across this every day in the parishes as she talked at length with unconvinced priests; and Father Hopkinson had taught her that this would be so. What she had not been prepared for were the deeper insights into the world of the prophets and visionaries which her work afforded her. These were the things which she could not discuss with any-one, for it seemed that there really was no-one in her Church who believed in their existence. With Iulia, she could hold the most rational of conversations about the most irrational of sub-jects. She wondered why she had not thought of her before.

It was Iulia who had recently come across Gilbert Shaw working in the east end of London among the poor and home-less. She had not been told that he dealt with 'possessions', but she knew that he practised the ministry of deliverance. You only had to meet him, to know, she said. After they had talked for almost half an hour, she turned to her address book and found his number for Noel.

Another phone call later and Noel had arranged to meet Father Shaw the following day at Liverpool Street Station. 'How shall I know you?' she had asked, to be told in reply 'Don't worry, I shall know you.' To her astonishment, this was indeed the case. Standing on the bridge, in the midst of a stream of people and smoke, they spotted each other as he looked up. It could not have been anyone else, he was so utterly distinctive. Standing well over six feet, he had 'shining white hair and piercing eyes'. Within a very short space of time, she felt as though they had known one another for years, such was their understanding. She left London that day, know-ing that she had found an ally.

From that point on, they worked on endless cases together. Whenever she came across something she couldn't handle or didn't understand, he would take the train down to Dorset and work with her. More often, they wrote to one another; long, long letters, his in spidery handwriting, each letter complete in itself as it explained some aspect of prayer or of the spirit-ual life. Wonderful gems of teaching almost impossible to decipher. He seemed to know instinctively when she wanted to talk and would suddenly appear at the station, demanding lunch. Then they would sit in her kitchen and talk for hours until the difficulty had been resolved; whereupon, he left as swiftly as he had arrived. In return, he enrolled her as one of his intercessors and took her with him whenever he came across a case of possession in her area; either person or building. His belief in the power of contemplative prayer was paramount. Noel never entered the building where the exorcism took place, she was asked simply to stand outside and to pray.

It was Gilbert who taught her about 'tuning in' from a distance and about protecting oneself from the harmful elements of healing. He had no time for anyone who allowed themselves to take on the symptoms of their patient's illness, and would constantly chivvy Noel about her exhaustion. He allowed her to believe that she had some measure of control over these things; and showed her how to attribute to the supernatural only that which properly belonged to it. 'You can do without getting exhausted and you can do without taking on others' symptoms. So do without it. And sink yourself in prayer.' He was a gentle man, but categorical, because he knew what he was talking about. Coming from a family that had always been categorical, Noel understood his approach and they met on an even front. He saw his purpose as one of insulating her with his prayer, of armouring her against the malign forces that were as much a part of healing as the good ones. It was his understanding of these things which taught her the most. The very fact that he took them seriously was to her a breath of fresh air. That he knew how to handle such matters and could be so eminently practical on the subject was what she respected him for the most. Her own experience had taught her to take the supernatural seriously, and she could not understand a Church who gave her the go-ahead in healing but would not even acknowledge the possibility of possession. Gilbert simply asked her to read the Gospels again, and she was comforted. Father Hopkinson had given her the theological basis and taught her about doctrinal observance: Gilbert taught her to listen to the Spirit. Father Hopkinson had trained her in the discipline of healing; she had needed to have tremendous discipline to continually be at the beck and call of anyone at any time in any part of the diocese. To be prepared, without a backward glance, to go to them and whatever you met there. It would have been hard as a nurse, but she was not carrying anything with her but the Spirit. Gilbert taught her how to be guided by the Spirit so that her reliance upon it became a source of strength and not a drain of energy. He recovered for her the sense of mystery which the institutional had gradually drained away since she was a child.

At the time that she got to know him, Gilbert Shaw was still considered highly suspect by the mainstream Church. Yet, whenever one came across the supernatural and needed help and advice, he was the first name on everyone's lips. He had suffered badly from being marginalised and rejected by the institution, but as he turned seventy he was facing the future with new optimism. Finding Noel was part of this new hope: in her he had someone who not only understood and respected him, but who could work with him whenever he needed assistance. He used her not only as an intercessor, but also for her literary skills. She skilfully edited his poetry[16] and meditative material where most people stumbled to understand the meaning. Where he was too uncertain even to offer his manuscripts to close friends and family, he handed them to her joking that she had better hold onto the mantelpiece if she couldn't keep her feet on the ground. She likened him to Teilhard de Chardin. He was the same sort of man, way beyond his time and not recognised by his Church. With him, as with no other director before him, she found herself getting right down into the depths and periodically right up to the top of the mountain. With Mary Clare, she had her teacher in prayer. From Gilbert Shaw she inherited an incredible storm of knowledge on healing and the mystical; things not taught by the Church, but only available in the teachings of the saints. He taught her about herself; her skills and abilities, what she was capable of and what she should never put up with.

In Gilbert Shaw she had satisfied her most basic hunger for knowledge, as well as discovering the guidance and direction she had always yearned for. Every move she made was

With husband Donald Davidson at a polo match in Burma, 1937

Donald in the jungles of Burma, 1938

With Caroline in Australia, 1942

With Caroline, Chelsea 1947

In the office in Parliament Square, 1951

Mother Mary of Malling
Abbey, taken through
the grill of the enclosure
in 1951

Photo by Noel Wynyard

Dr. Sister Tressie of La Retraite 1983 as painted by Caroline Davidson-Brewer

'Great'.
Noel and great-grandchildren,
Zoë and Peter, Salisbury 2001

Photo by Tessa Kuin Lawton

carefully monitored and discussed. She was never in any doubt about how each case should be handled, what the upshot was, and where the people who called on her needed spiritual guidance. When Arthur Hopkinson died she grieved, with her family, at the loss of a very dear friend. But she did not feel bereft of the teacher she needed. In the hands of Mary Clare and Gilbert Shaw she weathered the death of William Anderson and the succession of a line of bishops who were not interested in the healing ministry. She handled the destruction of every case report she had ever written in a fire at the Bishop's Palace and coped with the steady increase in demand for her services.

When Mary Clare telephoned to ask if they might meet in London in November 1957, Noel was too busy to accept her invitation. As the Reverend Mother was on her way to the sister-house in Burwash and had to catch a connection, she would have very little time anyway. And then the talk of stations reminded Noel of her first meeting with Gilbert Shaw. She gave Mary Clare his number and suggested that they meet; promising her that he had no aversion to station encounters. She had no idea what a success this meeting was to be. Mary Clare missed her train as they spoke for four hours, finally catching the last train to Burwash. She rang Noel in great excitement that evening to thank her for the introduction. Gilbert wrote to her to record the momentous conversation they had had. Noel was delighted with their encounter. She knew each of them as profoundly charismatic people, fluent writers and talkers. They had enough in common to build a great friendship and enough humility to see how much they had to learn from each other. Even in those early days, she likened them to Teresa of Avila and St John of the Cross. Their friendship was indeed to produce some of the most extraordinary work on prayer and the contemplative life written within the Anglican tradition. Together, they were able to initiate a rediscovery by the Church of the solitary life and to raise the profile of the importance of contemplative prayer. By 1962, Gilbert took over as Warden of Fairacres and spent the last years of his life there.

The qualities which she so admired in her mentors, proved

to be the same qualities which ultimately led to her separation from them. Mother Mary Clare and the nuns at Fairacres gave Gilbert new direction to his life and, with his usual single-mindedness, he turned his attentions to them. From then on his letters to Noel decreased gradually and his visits stopped. He no longer called her to work alongside him and all his correspondence about prayer was directed to Fairacres. At the same time, Noel found that the invitations to go to Oxford came less frequently than before. When Mary Clare needed someone to talk to the nuns about healing, she called on Gilbert rather than Noel. Little by little, the truth dawned on Noel that the close guidance and support on which she had come to rely so completely, was being removed. For the first time since she had begun this spiritual journey, twelve years ago, she was entirely on her own two feet. She had received the very best spiritual education and guidance she could have hoped for, from two of the greatest figures in the Anglican Church. Not a bad start in life, she thought. Now it was time to see just what she had learned.

13

THE PATTERN OF NOEL'S HEALING MINISTRY

For there is hope for a tree if it be cut down, that it will sprout again and that its roots will not cease.

Job 14:7

In retrospect, the gradual withdrawal of Noel's two spiritual mentors began a new chapter in her life. At the time, she simply coped with the fact; throwing herself into her work with new vigour, finding solace in a constant stream of other people. The work in the diocese was increasing every week. Among the parishes she was known as the face of the Church's healing ministry. At the same time, her ties with the institutional level of the Church were becoming less and less tight.

The informal and experimental nature of her role meant that she was free to pursue her job in spite of the attitude of different bishops towards healing. Each time a new bishop arrived she would take her letter of commission and explain the nature of her role. While no man ever rescinded this commission, there was none with whom she worked as closely as William Anderson. Some offered her their support, many agreed to allow her to continue, but none seemed to share the vision of Anderson. He had been a man ahead of his time; yet now that that time seemed to be dawning, the leaders of the Salisbury diocese were not anxious to capitalise on the experiment he had initiated and which continued at the grass roots of the diocese. While the 1958 Lambeth Conference was hearing the findings of a Commission on the ministry of healing, the fruits of an earlier bishop's labour were becoming visible. Like so many resolutions, however, those of the 1958 Conference were left to gather dust for another two decades[17].

Healing may now have been on the official agenda, but it was still little understood and deeply mistrusted by many of the clergy. Fox's classic on *The Church's Ministry of Healing* (Longmans 1959) helped to explain some of the history of these phenomena, but for too many of the Church's leaders this movement of the spirit was still not a reality. Meanwhile, at parish level, lay-workers such as Noel knew that it was a reality whose impact would soon be felt by all in authority. She relished the underground nature of her work; meeting people one-to-one, cell-to-cell. It gave her the chance to talk to them at length and discover what the laity of the Church of England really had on their minds at this time. She never ceased to be amazed both by the lack of opportunity for the laity to talk about their faith in this manner and at the way in which they embraced the notion of healing. It mattered not whether they were wealthy or poor, educated, or manual workers. Every one of them had a deep fund of knowledge about their faith, and a strong desire to talk about it. The power of the spirit to bring healing was indiscriminate.

The pattern of her ministry was to meet the person who had requested her help, usually in their home. Occasionally the priest would join them for this meeting, but the routine was that they should not be called until the service was conducted. After a long drive to get to the parishioner's house, Noel was always grateful for a cup of tea. In solid English tradition, this was the first step to relaxing the awkwardness between two strangers. Most people, she learnt, are anxious to talk about their illness and it did not take long for her to persuade them to do so. The most important part of Noel's job was to listen, and this could take a long time.

After allowing them to talk themselves into silence, she would introduce the stories of Christ's healing, with which they were familiar. Their difficulty lay in being able to relate a story 2,000 years old to their present situation. The majority of those with whom she talked understood their faith in direct relation to their church attendance. Thus their experience of faith was usually limited to their experiences in worship. It seemed true to say that in most cases worship had become a historical recounting rather than a living reality. As she prayed with them, Noel tried to bridge this gap and give them some insight into the God she knew. A Creator who desired that each created being should be whole and well, so that they might live in harmony with the rest of the natural world. She explained that the power that had made Jairus's daughter whole, and had healed the woman of her haemorrhage, was a force still working throughout creation today. When the spirit first moved across the waters of creation, God had set in motion a process, not a finite project. The natural order was still infused with the spirit: a spirit of life and energy which existed to balance the destruction and disintegration of the world. She told them stories of people today who had realised this inspiration and how it had affected their illness. She banished all thoughts that God wanted them to suffer and promised that it was the intention of the Creator to restore a sense of purpose and hope to those who were sick. The talking alone began this process within them, and Noel recognised the strength and importance of the ministry of listening. She wondered how many of the people whom she met were suffering primarily from loneliness. Her travels with the Village Evangelists had introduced her to the disintegration of the community, and had convinced her of the need for the Church. Now, she discovered that the Church itself was failing as 'community'. The congregations could not become more than an audience if they only met together once a week on Sunday. The health of the body of Christ was at risk because it was not addressing the whole. The isolation of many of these people was compounded by their nervousness in addressing God. If their faith was the Church, and the Church played no more than a superficial role in their lives, it followed that they were not able to gain the real sustenance which faith could provide. Noel's visits were times of listening and prayer. So often, she found herself discussing their communication with God and helping the parishioners to pray. Her years of learning with Mary Clare were passed on to anyone who wished to know more; and she was struck once again by the intimate connection between the contemplative and the practical. What greater nourishment to the ailing spirit was there? What greater hope for a spirit which must sustain a broken body than one which was feeding daily from the source. Why was no-one teaching the laity to pray?

Noel refused to countenance the idea that people's illnesses were directly proportional to their state of faith, rejecting the concept of faith healing which was now becoming popular. Some of the greatest saints who ever lived were those who had borne untold suffering. However, she wanted to reiterate her belief that what God wants is for people to be healthy. She always feared the inevitable question which every parishioner asked: will I get better? Worse, she feared their dissatisfaction with her answer: if God wills. She wanted to know what *they* wanted to know: why might it *not* be the will of God? She tried to move them away from the simplistic approach of 'healed' or 'not healed', towards an understanding of the source of strength which lay within them, waiting to be fed by prayer.

These were the times when she missed her mentors the most, but they were also the times when she understood how much she had learned from them and how much she had to give to other people. After years of leaning towards the contemplative and the scholastic, her work was now leading her into quite another sphere. Brother Edward had introduced her to it when he insisted she join him on the missions to Camelford and Eggbuckland. He had shown her that the quickest way to find God is to talk to the man in the street, studiously ignoring her preference for solitude and reconnecting her with the outside world. He had shown her that the journalist's desire to discover what makes a person tick cannot be completely fulfilled by maintaining a veneer of impersonal objectivity. With unremitting perseverance he breached the distance which she used to protect herself. Her friendship with

Jane, from Camelford, was just the beginning. Gilbert Shaw had shown her how to maintain an equilibrium between involvement and professional detachment; a balance which allowed her to learn more than she thought possible from those for whom she worked. In this hidden ministry, it was her privilege to meet a vast cross-section of people as she travelled the length and breadth of the diocese; and it was these people who taught her what her job was really about. The training she had received from Father Hopkinson was the foundation without which she could not begin to build, but it was the laity who taught her the meaning of the healing ministry. Given the opportunity, they could talk theology with more urgency and relevance than any master of the subject. With no publicity to herald her arrival, and no preconceptions of the work she did, they were interested and articulate. Each one knew their Bible and was full of questions.

At home, she involved herself as widely as possible in all aspects of healing. She joined the Institute of Religion and Medicine at the Salisbury Infirmary and read whatever was available in this field. She noticed how often she came across parishioners who needed more help than she could give them, those who would not be helped by a service of healing because they needed direct medical or psychological assistance. Her work in the hospitals led her further into a field in which she wanted to expand, but the experimental and freelance nature of the job gave her no freedom to do anything other than administer to the immediate spiritual problem. There was little room for long-term follow-up (although she always left her telephone number and dealt with more calls than she could handle). She could make recommendations to the parish priest, if he was open to them, but there was no link with the medical community. She wanted to be able to make some kind of diagnosis of the people who asked her to help, so that she could both pray directly for their needs and help them in a practical way by conferring with the local medical establishment.

Noel had always been puzzled and bothered by the fact that she never knew whether or not these people would get better.

'If the Lord wills it' was no help at all! But having a diagnosis of some sort would help. Whenever she had the opportunity to talk with sympathetic doctors, she took it; always searching for the borderline between the spiritual and the scientific. Gilbert Shaw had spoken to her of the nature of her gift; introducing her to the world of mysticism and the spiritual. In a letter he had written, explaining her 'special gifts', he told her

> GOD has given you this delicately balanced and intensely sensitive make up which lies mid-way between the spiritual and the psychic, and it does mean that your capacity to tune into spiritual and psychic forces will always be just beyond what your physical and mental powers will probably be able to hold onto, unless they are very carefully brought down to earth as well as tuned in to GOD.

Her years with Arthur Hopkinson, Mary Clare and Gilbert himself, meant that it was her instinct to centre all her experiences in God; however, it was these same people who had encouraged her inquisitiveness and restlessness with the status quo, both in their approach to her and in their theology. Theirs was a discipline which talked of the unseen as if it were the seen, which accommodated the mystery of God as much as it spoke of God's accessibility. They could not accept mere manners as a substitute for Christianity and taught her always to reach for the unattainable. Every day she was struck by the majesty of a being who had created the world and was the architect of the grand plan behind it all. She took nothing at face value.

The more involved she became with her work, the more she realised that much of the answer was found in an ability to identify with the sick. This was what enabled her to become so close to the parishioners who had called for her; this was what Brother Edward had begun. Gilbert Shaw traced it back to her 'Celtic roots' and talked of it as an awareness which the 'Celts are unable to avoid'. 'They are born into it,' he said, 'and it remains with them for life.' He spoke as an Irishman who knew, and she indulged his blarney! Years after they had parted, she would recall his certainty: the belief that those with this ability would recognise each other instantly. She remembered her own meeting with Gilbert and the life-changing meeting he had had with Mary Clare. She remembered her experiences in Australia when she had lived on a ranch with Donald; her close connection with the Aborigines. Perhaps there were whole peoples who were closer to the mysteries of the world than most. With a mind which rejected such philosophising more easily than accommodating it, she preferred to see it as a gift which was further developed during her work in intelligence, during the war. Such work was secret, sentient. Always one had to be one jump ahead of the next person, the next operation. She had been recommended for such work because of her work with Donald in the Burmese jungle[18].

In such a hostile environment she developed an extra sense against danger. Intelligence work fine-tuned such a gift, but it was not until her introduction to Gilbert Shaw that she understood the nature of her 'sixth sense'. Even then, he had only been able to give her an outline of the possibilities which lay ahead. It was in the rooms of those to whom she listened that she began to realise those possibilities. This profound degree of empathy allowed her to discern particular symptoms which the parishioners had not previously been able to articulate. She longed for the chance to work with the medical establishment so that the help she offered did not have to end with the articulation of symptoms.

However, Noel's work had begun as an experiment and was still regarded by most of the Church establishment as such. While the 1958 Commission had helped to legitimise this ministry to the sick, it was still an area full of uncertainty and misapprehension. Noel herself had been amazed by what she did not know as she immersed herself in the daily practice of the ministry. After several years of intensive learning she was only just beginning to discern the possibilities which the healing ministry might offer. She was at the cutting edge of this ministry and had to expect that her continuing experiments would be closely observed but rarely supported. Any links she wished to uncover between the spiritual and the scientific would have to be pursued alone.

14

DOWSING

Thou didst set the earth on its foundations so that it should never be shaken.
Thou didst cover it with the deep as with a mantle:

Psalms 104:5–6

As her understanding of the nature and extent of her role within the diocese was clarified, Noel became aware of the need to consolidate her financial position. James had retired from the Army soon after the War and his Army pension left very little room for manoeuvre. Convinced as she was by the need for the work which she was doing, she had yet to persuade anyone in the Church to back her either with a wage or expenses. She knew what was involved in setting up from scratch, and she looked around now for a means of earning an income which would not interfere with her work. Since leaving London, she had continued to write for the national press, and her contributions to some of the leading political journals of the day were accepted with gratitude but for a very small fee. The travelling in Dorset and Wiltshire ate into her time to the extent that reviewing was no longer possible. Writing was not the avenue for which she was looking.

The solution came to her at a time when she had almost run out of ideas. On a balmy summer evening, after almost eight years in the house she had designed herself, a couple in their early sixties came knocking at the door. They had taken their annual holiday in Chideock for the past decade and had watched the erection of the beautiful house by the orchard, with interest. Each year on their return to London they had promised that they would call in and meet the owners, but this was the first time they had plucked up the courage to do so. Dr Patten was retiring in the autumn and they had decided to look in Chideock for a suitable home. From the first day of her marriage to Donald, Noel had adopted an itinerant lifestyle and eight years was as long as she had spent in one place since then. She straightened her shoulders and invited the Pattens inside. As she and James prepared the drinks, the plan was outlined and agreed between them. By the end of the evening a settlement had been reached.

Their first move was to the delightful cedarwood bungalow in the orchard which she had designed at the time of the lay Order. Both Noel and James were astonished at the price they were able to command for the house and began to think about property investment more seriously. After two years they sold the orchard and bungalow and moved to the Marshwood Vale, where a prime piece of land was on offer at a ridiculously low price because it had no apparent water supply. When viewing the land, they felt so strongly that they would live there, Noel decided to practice a skill she had first learnt in Australia: dowsing.

During the War, friends of Donald's had invited her to stay at their sheep ranch in the outback. It was in late summer, after the longest drought they had experienced for years. The husband of the couple walked out across the dry fields, watching the sheep digging at the ground in an effort to get at the roots of the grass. Within the week, he knew he would lose a significant proportion of the flock. He invited Donald's wife to join him to 'come and see if we can get some water for these poor devils'. Holding a crowbar at arms length, he walked across the parched earth, looking for water. Noel kept a respectful distance, biting her lip at the humour of the scene. She was taken completely off guard when the crowbar began to quiver in his hands as if it were a frail stick. He marked the spot, took a spade, and dug until he found water. Enough to divert into a trough for the animals. Enough to keep them alive for another week. As she was digesting this extraordinary event, he handed her the crowbar and told her that she could do it too. Accepting the instrument with a calm she did not feel, she walked with him across the land. True enough, the thing dipped. Where it dipped and hit the ground they dug; and there they found water and put down a bore.

It was not so much the discovery of the water as the discovery of her own ability to divine it, which threw Noel. Her stay on the ranch was extended by another six weeks and the two of them discussed dowsing and its ramifications for most of that time. Dick had been practising it since he was a young man; it was a skill which his father and grandfather had passed on to him. He knew that many of the outback farmers used it as a necessary tool for the climate in which they lived. He did not see it as supernatural or peculiar, indeed his whole approach was practical and logical. His wife, Durlene, believed that the Aborigines understood a more complete picture of which dowsing was only a part. Essentially, dowsing is a skill which many more people are capable of than they believe. Most of the time they are prevented by their own disbelief. As she would soon learn, the theories about the nature of dowsing were as various as those who had discovered the ability to practise it. They were roughly divided between those who believed it was scientific, a tuning-in to the properties of water and minerals, and those who believed it was tuning in to some basic force of nature. What was certain was that the divining rod (whether it be stick, crowbar or other instrument) acted as a focus. The person who is sensitive enough to pick up the 'signals' (be they physical or etheric) used the divining rod as a kind of antennae. Dick was uninterested in the theories. He was concerned about one thing: whether or not his sheep were going to die. Only Noel's experience in Burma and the very ordinariness of her friend inclined Noel to accept something which was in all other ways so unorthodox. The fact that she could dowse was not what troubled her; it was more a question of whether she *should*.

It was Gilbert Shaw who showed her how to gather together

97

so many of her extrasensory experiences and explain them in language. He had put names to many of the things which she had been unwilling to acknowledge. The relief she felt in discovering a respected mentor who took such things seriously was tempered only by his own warning of the real danger of the field into which they were entering. The 'supernatural' was merely a word for those things which were outside the usual experience of the majority of people. As a result it was both misunderstood and subject to an unhealthy voyeurism by those who wanted to experience it by proxy. This led to a pressure which many of the minority (he called them 'sensitives') were unable to cope with. It was an interesting fact that not everyone who had access to this ability was emotionally or spirituality equipped to cope with the relationship between the two worlds. Under such external pressure, the first thing which was affected was their discernment. In the world of the unknown, the faculty of discernment is a more important skill than the gift of perceiving the supernatural. Gilbert taught her this from the first day he met her. He believed that full awareness of the dangers of the supernatural was the best possible means of humility in the face of such mystery. This, coupled with his insistence that they would always be a tiny minority in organised religious circles, kept Noel on the right side of orthodoxy. Her attitude of scepticism and rationality was the correct one and she should never renounce it. He agreed that there was nothing unseemly in a Christian healer practising dowsing, and she maintained her membership of the British Society of Dowsers (BSD), first obtained on return from Australia.

At the plot in the Marshwood Vale, she picked up a forked stick and walked the length and breadth of the land. Although she would never attempt to say how much flow or how deep the water was, she soon found what felt to be a large area of underground water close to the surface. With interest in the site still at a minimum, she took a chance and bought it at cost. She then called the Dorset Water Authority in Poole to come and investigate. Within the week, one of their service engineers was able to confirm, with the help of an old map, that they had found the source of the river Char. The house which she and James built there, Lambert's Corner, was the first in a long line of properties from which they earned their income. Noel always looked for local craftsmen and used them either to build a house or to renovate one. They would then live there until such time as their capital was running low or the market was too good to refuse a sale. In this way, she funded the project which had been initiated by the Bishop but never financially recognised by the Church.

It was during her time at Lambert's Corner that Noel found herself on the receiving end of a thoroughly debilitating illness. In the first two years of her healing ministry in the diocese, she had frequently developed the symptoms of those with whom she was working. Gilbert had shown her that she needed to protect herself against this with prayer. Other than this, she found she was rarely ill. So, this was unusual. Even the diseases of the tropics had not reduced her so low. She was taken into hospital at Axminster with a haemorrhage of the stomach. After a fortnight of tests and bedrest, she found herself recovered and was therefore discharged, despite no secure diagnosis of the complaint. Within a month of returning to Marshwood, she was rushed back to hospital with the same condition. This went on for several months; each time an apparent recovery was followed by a swift relapse. Finally, as she was about to be discharged for the fourth time, Dr Morton took her aside to talk to her. They had known each other for many years now, and as a Christian he had some respect for the work she did in the diocese. He certainly did not think it impossible that she should understand some aspects of the science of health which presently baffled the medical establishment. What he was surprised by was that she too seemed completely at a loss to diagnose herself. Before she returned to Marshwood, he begged her this time to apply herself to her own situation. Without wanting to frighten her, he felt there really was nothing more they could do.

The answer came to Noel when was sitting in a chair by the window, watching white pigeons wash themselves in puddles. Dr Morton's comments were occupying her mind once again as she considered the question of diagnosis. She was turning over the parishioners' question again and again, 'will I get better?' Why was it that a healer was able to act as a medium for God, yet was so rarely able to pinpoint the nature of the illness; to talk about it in human terms? Was the Church limited to the spiritual or was the spiritual in fact an integral part of the material? She felt the pain of division between two disciplines which were rendered weaker by their separation. If she was able to discern the presence of water by dowsing, there must be some way in which she could dowse her own illness. As she mulled these things over, her attention was caught by the pigeons. 'Why is it that they are well while I am so ill?' she thought. 'We share the same elements which constitute our existence.' There was nothing in the food she ate which made her ill, because at the time she was barely eating more food than a pigeon. The air she breathed was the same, the fire of the sun was the same. But the water... She drank the water from a well which she had sunk, and which had been tested for purity by the Water Board. She reached across for a book which a friend had sent to her when her illness had begun. Called *Fringe Medicine*, by Brian Ingils, it contained a number of interesting theories which were not normally found among the orthodox medical community. One such was called radiesthesia, a discipline which relied on a pendulum for diagnosis of illnesses. The book described it as 'dowsing for illness with a pendulum in order to achieve a diagnosis'. Noel had seen the pendulum in use before, and was keen to find out how it worked. If her theory about the connection between the water and her illness was correct, perhaps the pendulum could confirm the detail. She filed through the lengthy index of the book to the nearest practitioner; Mabel Lloyd in Somerset.

THE HEALING MOVEMENT

15

INVESTIGATIONS

. . . and the spirit of God was moving over the face of the waters.
Genesis 1:2b

Mabel Lloyd was in her eighties when Noel was first introduced to her in 1964. A small but significant woman, she lived alone in a beautiful, draughty house in the village of Queen Camel in Somerset. There she played a fine hand of bridge, continued to ride to hounds, and drove a Sunbeam Rapier. As soon as they met the two women fell into the easy conversation of those with many things in common. Most importantly, Noel related to someone who was ordinary, in the sense that she enjoyed so many of the worldly pleasures of her class.

With a printed leaflet which explained the *Radiesthesic Therapy* practised by Mabel Lloyd, Noel walked around the office and diagnosis room, taking in the rows of neatly organised files full of case histories. She thought back to the time when she had to write up every case she came across and send it to the Bishop, and respected this bluff old woman all the more. Such recording required meticulous dedication.

From their conversations, it quickly became clear that Mabel would not regard this stranger as one of her patients. Rather, she wanted to introduce her to the methodology of radiesthesia and allow Noel to learn how to diagnose and treat herself. Confirming Gilbert Shaw's belief that sensitives can recognise one another, she had not needed to be told that her

103

new patient was a dowser. Before she learnt the whole story, she explained her art in the simplest possible terms.

Radiesthesia is known also as medical dowsing. The tool used in this case is not a stick or crowbar, but a pendulum. This is a small heavy object on the end of a short piece of string. The object itself is largely irrelevant to the action it performs; Mabel's was made of ivory and shaped into a fine point at the end. Not everyone capable of dowsing can use a pendulum accurately and, in the same way, those who have not learned how to dowse may well be able to use the pendulum. It is held lightly in the hand between forefinger and thumb, and kept still. The user concentrates the mind and asks a question which can be answered 'yes' or 'no'. The pendulum should begin to swing in one of two directions: forward and back, or round in cyclic motion. Each user will know which is yes and which is no, but it varies from person to person. It is believed that, in the same way a stick dips or moves when it comes into contact with the substance it has been asked to locate, the pendulum 'picks up' something in the atmosphere, directly related to the person about whom one is asking questions. In dowsing circles, as Noel knew well from the conferences and BSD journal, it was generally believed that what the dowser was registering was a force, or power of nature; probably radiation rays. Radiesthesia was the use of dowsing to diagnose illness and to determine the remedies which would be able to treat it. To put it another way, it was a way of 'using the faculty of dowsing to analyse and measure the same "force of nature" in the disease pattern (ie the diagnosis) and in the same way to determine the remedies which would correct this pattern (ie the treatment)'.[19] Those able to use a pendulum were those who were particularly sensitive to the forces of nature which made dowsing possible.

When she had first experienced dowsing in Australia, Noel had found the whole process quite extraordinary. If it were not for the fact that it worked, and that those around her who used it were so ordinary, she would have tried to forget it. As it was, the empirical evidence joined forces with her scepticism and ensured that she read as much as she could about the phenomenon; in an attempt to understand the inexplicable. When, later she came to healing, she was less surprised by the extraordinary, not least because healing could be fitted into the framework of her faith; a faith which had come to accept the mysterious as a fundamental facet of the divine. She did not make an explicit connection between dowsing and healing, but neither did she find them incompatible. Her faith had always been rooted in its appreciation of a Creator God and the ongoing process of a remarkable creation. The ministry which she had been able to bring to so many was evidence to her of the deep desire for this Creator to be reconciled with humanity, and for humanity to live in harmony with nature. She did not believe that nature could be addressed objectively, and always associated it with creation; however, she was certain that the healing power unleashed by the Holy Spirit was an integral part of that creative force which was constantly at work in nature. She believed that the power of the Spirit was the wellspring of all the forces of nature which were at work in the world. In the same way that she had been taken unawares by the magnetic pull of the crowbar to hidden water and the force of the blessing which came through her hands, she recognised that there might be a plethora of unseen elements which the world was reluctant to reveal. Her years with Gilbert Shaw had taught her to keep an open mind about such things. He had, however, also taught her to be on her guard, to investigate such things thoroughly and *always* to offer them to God.

At the time that Noel and Mabel Lloyd met, radiesthesia was still a very new discipline. It had been first developed in France by monks, the Abbé Mermet and the Abbé Boulay. The 'force of nature' which it was believed the pendulum picked up on, was radiation. In the knowledge that all matter radiates, it was thought that the pendulum might be 'catching' the radiation. A person's health could be measured by the amount that person was radiating. Not surprisingly, in an age dominated by mankind's knowledge of the physical laws which govern the material universe, there was a need both from those who practised this new art, and those outside, to establish some sort of scientific basis for radiesthesia. The founders of the Medical Society for the Study of Radiesthesia were all part of the medical establishment[20] and those who followed their lead were anxious to place this new discipline squarely in a scientific framework. Thus Abrams in the United States, and De la Warr in England, searched for scientifically-based methodologies of radiesthesia. The former created 'Abrams box', which used a small black box to transmit the radiation of the practitioner to the patient. The latter devised a system of 'rates' which measured the radiation dowsed in each person. Everything was supposed to have its rate, expressed in a number. This was the method which Mabel used. She would use the pendulum to diagnose which part of the body was at the root of the illness. This would give her a rate with which to work. She would then look up the remedy which such a rate required and would offer it to the patient. Noel asked her the origin of the theory of rates and began to read up on Abrams and De la Warr. When talking with Mabel about it on a later visit, she discovered that there was no one centralised method used. Each worker in this field used their own technique. Thus, both the readings which the pendulum gave them, and the rates which were attributed to each illness, were different for each person. Such a confusion of diversity was enough to make Noel sceptical of rates. She did not believe that the use of the pendulum, to which she had quickly adapted, had to be tied to this particular methodology. She was fascinated by the movement which had sprung up round this medical dowsing, but was not convinced enough by their method to wish to take on the whole discipline.

The pendulum, on the other hand, made a great deal of sense and worked well for her. It was so similar to dowsing that she hardly felt she was embarking on anything new. The technique was universal and very simple. The first case she diagnosed was her own, as Mabel had expected it would be. She considered the treatment she had received at the hospital and the revelation she had received when watching the pigeons in the puddles outside her window. Thinking it through carefully, she worked out a series of questions to use with the pendulum in order to reach some kind of conclusion about the cause of the illness. It took very little time to discover that her suspicions had been correct: perhaps there was something in the well at Lambert's Corner which was attacking the lining of her stomach. Having originally had their water tested for purity, she now called the Water Board and asked them to come and test it for metals. The result was an unusually high level of copper. Enough to do serious damage to someone with a sensitive stomach, and to explain some of the occasional problems James had been suffering from. Jubilant, she rang both Dr Morton and Mabel Lloyd. Each one offered to prescribe a remedy, but she already knew what she wanted to do. For a few months she ate only enough to keep her going. Her main diet consisted of local cream, taken in teaspoons at regular intervals, in order to re-line the wall of her stomach. Dr Morton was highly cynical of this diet but, watching her progress from six stone to eight, made no further comment.

Mabel was delighted by this first success. It was not her habit to see people privately, but she liked Noel and felt that in her she might have discovered someone who could carry the torch when she was no longer able to work. Although there was very little discussion of her healing ministry, Mabel was certain that this person had the sort of potential which one did not come across often. She appreciated a quick brain and an open mind and particularly enjoyed the fact that Noel was not shy about speaking her mind when the two women disagreed. They talked for long hours about the kind of patients Mabel had seen and the sort of illnesses they suffered from. She was introduced to the work of some of the great practitioners and met De la Warr in Oxford. There were entertaining hours when she learnt about the practice of radiesthesia on horses! Mabel was a permanent physician to the Duke of Norfolk's horses and did many remarkable cures on them.

After almost eighteen months of time spent at Queen Camel, Mabel handed her most precious pendulum to Noel, telling her to 'carry on and use it well'. Back at Lambert's corner the story was recounted to James and the tiny instrument held up for his inspection. 'Do you know, I think she has taught me everything she knows,' she said, playing with her unexpected gift. When the telephone rang early the next morning, she knew that Mabel was dead before James broke the news to her.

16

ANALYSIS AND PROJECTION

The Lord sits enthroned over the flood; the Lord sits enthroned as
*   King for ever.*
May the Lord give strength to his people! May the Lord bless his
*   people with peace!*

                                                    Psalms 29:10–11

The chaotic relativism of the 1960s had more impact on Noel
than she would have believed at the time. For her, the decade
was characterised by a laity struggling with confusion as
their leaders retired into the solace of their own privacy to
grapple with the realities of post-enlightenment thought.
While Bishop Robinson and others opened wide the doors of
traditional Christian thought, their parishioners found themselves left behind. In Noel's experience it was not because they
were not able to cope with the content of the debate, but
rather that no-one had asked them to be involved. Her early
experience was of a silent majority with a thirst for spiritual
direction. The only difference that she witnessed as the decade
progressed, was a deepening confusion and the beginnings of
scepticism about those in authority. She found herself pulled in
two directions: on the one hand she was constantly being called
to reaffirm the truths which formed the basis of her belief
in the Church. Her mission to those she met was one of re-
assuring them of the existence of certain fundamental truths.
On the other, being bombarded with both their questions and

those of the Bishops was enough to register a certain shaking of the solid foundations with which she had been provided by Father Hopkinson. She yearned for a spiritual director with whom she could analyse such matters. One could not but be aware of theology in flux as never before. Noel knew that the time in which she was living was one of change at a pace faster than she had previously witnessed. She knew that the formulations which had schooled her were true, but she also knew that she would have to find new ways of expressing the same truths if she were not to lose hope of being understood by the parishioners she met.

She was not afraid to read the experimental theologies which the new relativism was producing, but she did not always feel able to grasp the full implications of their hypotheses. While so many around her stood, as if at the prow of a ship in full steam, all she could see was the density of the fog and wished for a quiet retreat from where she could watch and pray. In the absence of a director, she fell back on the tools she had been given, and comforted herself that in the Bible, when Jesus had ascended, the disciples no longer had his physical presence guiding and teaching them. They would have had to learn to rely on their own discernment and the Spirit. Her instinct was to rely on man more than God, and she had spent her life in the company of inspiring people. Now, when she needed them most, she found herself with no-one but God. It was far from comfortable but she had little choice. The psalms came to mean a great deal to her as she read the daily offices.

The Bishop who had succeeded William Anderson in 1963[21] had agreed, on meeting her, that Noel should continue her ministry within the diocese. On his accession she had hoped that the opportunity might be presented for the creation of a permanent position. She was not sure what she had in mind: the situation in Manchester with Helen Noble was a public statement of the Church's backing and support. Helen had one church from which she worked in close association with a team of others. However, Noel recognised that such an organisation could restrict her movement to one church and one or two priests. She had come to value the opportunity which travelling gave her to meet a wide range of parish priests and the insight she was privileged to glean of parish life from both its priests and its laity. Gilbert Shaw had once written to her that the

> pattern of your life since the Bishop gave his commission
> has been a difficult one for any woman ... As I see it you
> are doing three things at once: a) making your own con-
> tacts on a very wide scale involving real physical and
> spiritual strain on your journey's, b) converting the clergy
> – a whole job in itself, c) administering healing grace.

The latter was at the heart of her ministry and could, of course, have been located within a single frame of reference. It was the first two which she would lose if she were given a church from which to work, and she saw all three as integral to her ministry. The chance to meet people in their own homes or parishes was a gift; it allowed them to talk to her with the confidence of familiarity in an otherwise frightening situation. It gave her the freedom to offer the time that each person needed, to tailor each visit to individual circumstances. There was no difficulty with maintaining privacy, for the matter was always handled by no more than two or three people and, if a healing service were offered, it could be adapted for each case. She had visited and talked with Helen Noble and also with Dorothy Kerin[22]. She saw in them the same gift of healing grace, but was interested to note the different way in which it was being administered. They talked to her openly of the advantages of church support and public recognition, but gave her the confidence she needed to continue with the method initiated by Bishop Anderson. In the early post-war years, heal-ing was still struggling to be accepted by the mainstream Church and was having to carve out a path for itself. When these women talked, they acknowledged that the nature of the God who worked through them was such that there would never be one route, and wondered how this dynamic spirit might be organised into the human institution. Their discus-sions ranged primarily over the debate between the need for

111

order and boundaries, and the knowledge that the spirit of God could never be contained. Somehow a balance had to be sought between the Church, those with the gift of healing and the Spirit of God.

For herself, Noel felt that the cell-to-cell nature of her ministry was the right way forward. She came from a contemplative background where silence and space were integral to the experience of God. She could identify with the peripatetic ministry of Jesus and the privacy and intimacy which he seemed to crave with those whom he healed. When Bishop Fison agreed to see her to discuss her commission, she hoped that they could talk about these things and construct a way forward. To build not only on the experimental foundations laid down by his predecessor, but to devise a plan for development. It would be a risk, she knew, because this experiment was already moving in a very different direction to the healing ministry in other dioceses. What Noel had forgotten was that *in itself* healing was still regarded with a healthy suspicion by most of the leaders of the church. The Bishop was delighted to have met her and gave her his full blessing to continue with the commission. At the end of her meeting, however, she was as much of a free agent as she had been at the beginning.

Any sense of disappointment she felt at the time was buried beneath the demand for her work. Her most pressing concern was how to fund her ministry so that it might continue in the years to come. The volume of work and financial questions gave her no time to consider or assess the direction in which it was going. For five years she had continued with the pattern which had been established in the early days of her training: frequent travel and moving house almost every year. By 1968, however, Gilbert's warning about the exhausting nature of the work was starting to make itself felt. Each year, they had had to move into a smaller property in order to maintain an income from their capital.

It was Gilbert who had first introduced her to the notion that those who heal are always in danger of picking up the pain and suffering with which they are in contact every day. It is a select few who choose to confront the ugliest side of human circumstance. The gospels talk of 'power going out of Jesus' (Luke 8:46) and in their constant references to his retreat into the mountains give some hint of his need to recharge himself. Those with the gift of healing seem to understand this. Some have talked of immediate exhaustion after laying on hands, others are laid low with the symptoms of the diseases they have been asked to treat. Noel had been particularly susceptible to this, and Gilbert had been quick to show her how to protect herself with prayer. In simple form this must always be the answer: whether you work for the church or the medical profession, the cumulative effect of such exposure to suffering can be disastrous if you do not give yourself space to recover. For Gilbert Shaw, the reason why some were particularly affected was their sensitive make-up and the remedy of 'space' was always to be found through contemplative prayer. It was more than just a break, it was an integral part of one's spiritual journey. A letter he had written to her in 1958 had as much relevance a decade later as it had done at the time:

> Moreover there has been no time for you to grow and develop your spiritual consciousness and power by that quiet receptivity to GOD whereby He does give us that deep intuitive knowledge of Himself, which by the way, is itself an unfailing reservoir of spiritual power.

So, at the end of 1968 Noel took a much needed break on the Channel Island of Sark. The desire to step back from the world and observe, to find the space to pray and attend to her own faith was always strong; but now it became imperative. She was not ordained but she knew the trials of a minister. The greatest pleasure was also the greatest burden: the number of questions with which people confronted her, sometimes crowded her to the point of claustrophobia, leaving her no room for the questions and doubts which were part of her own spiritual journey. For almost a decade, she had been the face of the Church to these people. The weight of such responsibility was made bearable by the knowledge that, as a woman

113

in the 1960s, she had received an insight which few were accorded. When combined with the fact that her concern was exclusively with those *in extremis*, the insights were sometimes too painful to handle. At such times the crowd became something to be escaped from, so that she might later return. The advantage of her freedom was that it allowed her to make such a break.

17

A BRIEF HISTORY OF HEALING

Solitude is as necessary for society as silence is for language.
Thomas Merton

The Gospel writers themselves acknowledged that healing was not the prerogative of the Son of God or His followers (John 21:25). It was the use of his charismatic gift of healing, in the service of God and the proclamation of the Kingdom of God, which set Jesus apart from other healers. Even so, he was wary of misinterpretation and the gospels all testify to his healings within the context of his extraordinary capacity for compassion. Above all else, Jesus' healing ministry demonstrated the compassion of God for humanity. His involvement with people showed that the Kingdom of God would be characterised by such compassion: by the desire of God to see humanity restored to its proper harmony with the created order which God first recognised as 'very good' (Genesis 1:31).

During his ministry, Jesus appears to have been training both his disciples (Matthew 10) and a larger gathering of his followers (the 'seventy', Luke 10). He 'sent them out' to preach and heal. The equipment they carried with them was little more than his words of truth and the promise that if they prayed they would be heard (Matthew 6:9–13). The message which Jesus brought was of the Kingdom of God: what it was, what it would be like and what people should

115

do to make it a reality in this world. He taught his followers so that they could carry this message with them. He also taught them that there were those among themselves who could heal people in his name. It is not surprising then, that when Jesus had finally left them, his followers continued to pray, preach and heal as they had been taught. The Acts of the Apostles and all the epistles to the young churches are full of a dynamic vitality as they carry out Jesus' core commandments: to heal the sick, to love one another, to baptise all nations, and to do it all in remembrance of him. References in Justin Martyr, Tertullian, Irenaeus and Origen testify to a flourishing ministry of healing among the Christian community of the first three centuries.[23]

Most theologians trace the gradual sedimentation of this fast flowing stream to the conversion of the Emperor Constantine (fourth century). At this point, Christianity was confronted less with persecution than with the intellectually arduous task of accommodating the mechanisms and structures of power in the political world. By 313 the Edict of Milan confirmed a Church preoccupied with matters of institutional organisation and theological systematisation. Cyprian's fear that the Church lacked strength in prayer and was growing more worldly,[24] seems to have been borne out by the fourth century, despite the fact that 'God raised up some of the greatest minds to serve him in this period'.[25]

Belief in the miraculous was not incorporated into their theologies. Left to the realms of the superstitious, sickness and sin became integrally connected. The use of oil (unction) to bless and heal people became less and less frequent, until it came to be seen as 'extreme unction' and used only to ensure healing in the next life, rather than this one. Indeed, this approach has been reversed in the Latin Church only as recently as 1962, when the anointing with oil was reinstated as a sacrament of healing.[26]

It would be wrong to suggest that healing disappeared as part of the Christian life from Constantine's conversion and was then suddenly revived 1500 years later. What is accurate to say is that there are virtually no records which refer to healing.

Thus it is safe to assume that it was largely ignored within the hierarchies of church structure. However, as this century has shown with compelling force, healing is more often than not a gift given to the laity. There are striking examples, from the end of last century and the beginning of this, of the spirit of God working through particular individuals endowed with the charismatic gift of healing. Such gifts were not withheld from individuals from the fourth century onwards. Rather, they have coincided in this century with a broadening vision of those in authority in the Church, which has allowed their prophetic voices to be heard and considered by a greater number of people.

One of the individuals who made such an impact on the church was the layman James Moore Hickson. He was first commissioned by the Archbishop of Canterbury (Randall Davidson) in 1906. His charge was 'to go forward like the patrol of an army and come back and report'. He did this for eleven years, travelling ceaselessly up and down the country and using his peripatetic lifestyle to gather a unique picture of the state of the nation's spiritual health. In the same way that Jesus had prepared his followers by teaching them how to pray (Luke 11:1–13), Hickson saw that prayer was the basis of his ministry. He believed that he could not carry out his mission without the support of prayer, and asked wherever he went that parishes support his ministry through intercessory prayer for the sick.[27]

In 1917, during a period of withdrawal for prayer and quiet reflection on Iona, he came to understand God's plans for him abroad. Within a year he was travelling to the USA, Canada, India, China, Japan and the Philippines. In each place he would meet the Bishop of the diocese and ask for his commission to heal there. Wherever he held services of healing, he worked closely with the priests, thereby initiating a simultaneous process of converting the clergy.[28]

One of the more interesting facts about the apparent revival of the healing ministry is that the spirit has so often worked through laywomen. Thousands have converged on the shrines of Fatima of Portugal, Anne de Beaupré of Canada

117

and Bernadette of Lourdes. Dorothy Kerin was herself miraculously healed at the age of 23 and so began her lifetime's work. Unlike Hickson, she was not an itinerant, but gathered a group of loyal assistants around her and worked from within community hospitals in London, which she herself established. The pattern was replicated at Burrswood in Kent in 1948; the foundations so well laid that it still stands as testimony to her life's devotion to Christ the healer. Mention has already been made of Helen Noble in Manchester. Although very little has been written of her ministry, she was a pioneer in the establishment of healing as part of the mainstream, rather than a fringe activity. In Germany, Theresa Neumann worked tirelessly for those who came to her, while in the United States Kathryn Kuhlman's life followed a similar pattern. Also in the USA was Agnes Sanford, who came to be known to many through her books and the Schools of Pastoral Care. Each woman was 'found' by God and presented with a gift which then determined the rest of their lives. Noel heard little from any of them, but drew some comfort from the fact that she was not entirely alone.

At a formal level, one can trace the earliest impetus towards the reinstatement of healing into the mainstream church to 1904, when Dr Percy Dearmer formed the Guild of Health. The stated aim of the Guild was to encourage co-operation with the medical profession in the practice of healing: 'to help people experience within the fellowship of God's family the freedom and life promised by Jesus Christ and to enable all members to study the interaction between physical, mental and emotional factors in well-being, and their relationship with the spiritual life in prayer and meditation'. One of the healing groups affiliated to the Guild of Health was James Hickson's Society of Emmanuel, later called the Divine Healing Mission.

In 1915, when the Guild became inter-denominational, the specifically Anglican Guild of St Raphael was founded on the same principles of close association with the medical profession. The Guild of St Raphael was keen to maintain a sacramental basis to its organisation, and with the ecumenical movement no more than an embryonic vision, there were many Anglicans who feared that sacramental authority might be undermined by inter-denominational co-operation. Theologians associated with the Guild were anxious to place healing squarely within the mainstream sacramental work of the Church and its teaching, and their practice was

> that of the Lord Jesus Christ and His Apostles as revealed in the Gospel and handed down through all ages in Christ's Holy Catholic Church, ie by the Ministry of the Word, the Sacraments – especially the anointing of the sick – the Laying on of Hands and the faith of the Church as expressed in corporate and personal prayer.

At the heart of their movement was the belief that the clergy should have no reason to fear healing as an 'unknown'. They published a quarterly paper from their inception and watched it raised from a small leaflet to a publication of substance under the editorship of Prebendary Henry Cooper, from 1954. It was their small publication of the litany and office book which were most popular with clergy. Each booklet offered the chance to follow a set liturgy within a familiar framework. This gave the clergy greater confidence to work with laity like Noel. Conversely, it was a pattern familiar enough to the parishioners to allow them to relax. In recent times the liturgies of the Guild of St Raphael have become less popular. However, as Noel's own ministry adapted to these circumstances, she nevertheless found many priests, interested in healing but uncertain of their first step, who were extremely grateful for these booklets.

Within the leadership of the churches, there was some formal recognition of a growing movement among the laity. The Lambeth Conferences of 1908 and 1920 considered the subject and eventually agreed that 'the use with prayer of the laying on of hands, the unction the sick and other spiritual means of healing' be reported on. The committee's report was published in 1924 and concluded that 'the power to exercise spiritual healing is taught by Christ to be the natural heritage of Christian people who are living in fellowship with God, and is part of the ministry of the Church'.[29]

The report was commended by the bishops at the same time as they pressed for a growing co-operation between the doctors and clergy and the formation of regular intercessory prayer groups in each parish. Hickson's fundamental belief in prayer as the heart of the healing ministry was echoed by the conference.

It wasn't until 1944, under Archbishop William Temple, that these recommendations were moulded into the structures of a recognisable organisation concerned with the Churches' Healing Ministry. The first meeting of the Archbishop's Development Committee of the Guild of Health was held in Lambeth Palace on 21st April 1944. At the time, Godfrey Mowatt was the Archbishop's representative and was permitted to travel widely on his behalf. That he took these duties very seriously is testified to in the minutes of a meeting of 1947, when William Temple's successor recorded that 'Godfrey Mowatt is quite uncontrollable, both in the energy which he puts into his work, and in the variety of places he visits, and in the spirit of Christian love and peace that he carries about with him wherever he goes'. And this despite his total blindness. During one of his travels, Noel was introduced to Godfrey Mowatt. In much the same way as she had been inspired by Brother Edward and James Hickson, she found herself mesmerised by the dedication with which he pursued the itinerant lifestyle and she knew that it was also the right path for her to follow. When she had been working for a few years in the Salisbury diocese, Godfrey suggested to her that he might put her name forward as his successor. Quite apart from the question of whether the Church authorities would have accepted a woman in such a senior role, Noel realised that her calling was to the parochial diocesan rather than the national. Not only was it the best way successfully to combine work with married life, it also gave her a sense of community and continuity which provided the support she needed to maintain such a lifestyle. Mowatt continued to work alone until his death in 1958.

18

HEALING AND THE MEDICAL PROFESSION

Human beings were created who could paint, compose, write, play, laugh, cry, think, grow to love and worship their God and experience a fragile freedom, caught between this order and this randomness.

Bishop Jim Thompson, Synod, July 1996

In 1946, after William Temple's death, the committee came to be known as the Churches' Council of Healing (CCH). It was deeply involved in the relationship between healing and medicine, and in 1947 representatives of the Medical Committee had discussions with the Central Ethics Committee of the BMA. The BMA printed a two page statement about the CCH in the British Medical Journal, endorsing the importance of co-operation between the two. Mowatt's successor, Geoffrey Harding, also had an exhaustive programme of travelling and speaking engagements, but concerned himself chiefly with the relationship between clergy and doctors. It was he who proposed the establishment of the Institute of Religion and Medicine (IRM) which got off the ground in 1963, and whose local branch in Salisbury was so important to Noel. Thereafter, the Council became the mouthpiece for the Churches' Healing Ministry, submitting reports to the administrative bodies of the Churches,[30] producing publications,[31] and concerning itself with affiliated organisations such as the IRM, the Clinical Theology Association and the Hospital Chaplains' Fellowship.

122

Throughout her visits to parishioners, Noel had always stressed that God wanted people to be whole and well. God's purpose for humanity is health and not sickness. She would use stories from the Gospels to illustrate the point that Jesus' main objective while on this earth was the elimination of disease and the restoration of hope and purpose to people's lives. He seems to have shown the greatest concern for the physical and mental well-being of his followers. Yet, tragically, it was the Church which began the process of divorce between this faith in Christ and the practice of the healing arts. The first Lateran Council of 1123 forbade monks to visit the sick or administer unction. The studying of medicine in the monasteries was prohibited by the second Council in 1139 and twenty-four years later, in 1163, the Council of Tours forbade all church-men from practising surgery, with the dissection of the human body later being declared sacrilegious. It was not for many centuries that priests who were doctors were permitted to practice.

In this century, it seems that it has also been the Church which has made the first overtures towards the reconciliation of these two profoundly connected disciplines. In 1947 the BMA approved a statement on medicine and the Church which had been drafted after discussions between the Medical Committee of the Churches' Council for Healing and the Central Ethics Committee of the BMA:

Medicine and the Church working together should encourage a dynamic philosophy of health which would enable every citizen to find a way of life based on moral principle and on a sound knowledge of the factors which promote health and well-being. Health is more than a physical problem and the patient's attitude to both his ill-ness and other problems is an important factor in his recovery and adjustment to life. Negative forces such as fear, resentment, jealousy and carelessness play no small part in the level of both personal and national health. For these reasons we welcome opportunities in the future for discussion and co-operation between qualified medical

123

practitioners and all who have concern for the religious needs of their patients.

The co-operation between doctors and priests was something which the CCH was keen to establish from its inception. However, as Maddocks writes in his seminal work on the healing ministry (quoting Dr Kenneth Leese):

> [this] attempt at reconciliation proved to be in the nature of a 'bridge too far'. It was in some ways so far in advance of secular medical thinking as to be almost totally ineffective in its impact on the post-war physician. This ineffectiveness has deepened the gloom of those within the profession who, as avowed Christians, have seen in society a developing secularism with its concomitant new emphasis upon materialism; the pressures for time-demanding cures rather than true healing; the trivia of minor complaints, the disproportionate use of resources and the real danger of a loss of respect for the dignity of human personality in the pursuit of scientific advance.[32]

Noel would often find herself feeling exactly as Dr Leese described; involved as she was also with the 'scientific' concerns of dowsing and radiesthesia and yet alienated from so many of those who practised it alongside her. Her own preference was for a rigorous scientific approach, and she applauded those within the BSD who were so anxious to be seen as a mainstream medical discipline. Perhaps she was unusual, however, in her desire to want to see the combination of the methodology and approach of science with the openness to mystery and the transcendent which characterised religion. For surely this was the only way in which scientific information could be prevented from becoming the end rather than the means of serving humanity? She was concerned that healing and medicine were being impoverished by this unnatural divorce, but also yearned for evidence of a truly Christian perspective on such matters.

The Churches' Council for Health and Healing was

concerned with the healing of the relationship between medicine and the Church, from its inception. It was the vision of William Temple which initiated the establishment of the Council in 1944. He gave as its mandate the three main points of the 1920 Lambeth Conference report on healing:

1. That *teaching* on the Christian Healing Ministry should be given in the churches.
2. That *co-operation* with the medical profession should be sought at every level.
3. That an intercessory *prayer* group should be formed in every congregation.

After the publication of the statement in the BMA journal, CCH went on to spearhead several other initiatives in this field. As we have already noted, in 1963 the Institute of Religion and Medicine was formed under the guidance of CCH's Director, Geoffrey Harding. This was a national organisation which promoted the work of field groups at local level. During this time, the list of new member bodies of the Council gives a clear idea of its priorities: the Free Church Hospital Chaplain's Association, The Clinical Theology Association and the Institute of Religion and Medicine. A decade later, the Council sponsored the compilation of a directory of all the caring agencies in the field of health and healing.[33] This was followed several years afterwards with the sponsoring of a consultation on inter-professional referral at the Reading postgraduate medical centre.

At the same time as Noel was considering the relationship between religion and medicine, there were those in both disciplines calling for a shift in emphasis from the sick patient to the healthy individual; from the treatment of disease to the ideal of attaining a positive level of health. Part of this shift included moving from an arm's length relationship between professionals and their clients, to a personally shared experience. Maddocks echoes the method which Noel had developed over the years when he says: 'If those of us in the caring professions are really honest, we know that the people we have been able to help most have been those with whom we have identified as person to person and spent time with, listening patiently and diligently to what they are really saying'. The investigation of holistic medicine by the Church suggested that by widening the concept of health to include prevention as well as cure, it might be possible to open the doors to interdisciplinary dialogue and co-operation. This wider understanding of health might also inculcate a sense of responsibility among individuals both for themselves and for others; thereby eradicating the pervading belief that cures for sickness are the right of every person (the corresponding duty of the doctor being to dispense whatever treatment the latest drug company is advertising). Noel's experience in this regard was that any diagnosis necessarily had to include a way in which the person could leave feeling that it were possible to take responsibility for helping themselves. In order to achieve this, she had to be most careful to explain the nature of healing so that it was not seen as yet another 'quick fix' cure which provided a useful alternative to pills. She would talk of a God whose hope was that the kingdom could be brought about by ordinary people in ordinary situations; and that the establishment of the kingdom on earth began with those people taking care of themselves and those around them. God, she said, was at the heart of people's relationships with each other, and it was in the restoring of relationships that God's healing presence was most often found.

19

REFLECTION AND DECISION

I do not pray that thou shouldst take them out of the world, but
that thou shouldst keep them from the evil one.
They are not of the world, even as I am not of the world.
Sanctify them in the truth; thy word is truth.

John 17:15–18

When she returned from Sark, Noel was not entirely sure her state of mind was that which she might have hoped for when she envisioned her retreat. During her time away James' health which had been deteriorating for some time, had now reached a critical level and he was now in need of hospital treatment.

The first person within the diocese whom Noel contacted was Bishop Fison. He drove to Marshwood to hear about her experiences of healing in Sark and the present situation with James. It was agreed that she should try and continue with her ministry initially at a local level. Whether she broadened her work to the rest of the diocese depended on demand for it and her family circumstances.

As she got back to work she was surprised that there seemed to be no pause in the demand for her ministry of healing. Indeed, she had noted an apparent increase in people's awareness and acceptance of the ministry on her return to Dorset. Her sleepy village of Marshwood was now home to an active vicar keen to promote the charismatic healing movement. Her own preference in religion reflected a reserved and meditative character: she did not feel immediately comfortable with the style of worship which had been adopted in her parish and was not unhappy that her priest was already working closely with someone else. She was grateful to him for respecting their differences and pleased that he referred those people he thought would benefit from a one-to-one ministry to her.

It was wrong to believe that she held a patent on the healing ministry in Dorset, but perhaps she had been its sole representative for too long. A pioneer becomes used to the solitary way of life and draws succour from the unique position and others' dependence upon it. All the hours of careful listening and explaining are rewarded by the fact that you yourself are held in high regard. She had been aware of this danger and had always sought out the partnership of parish priests in an attempt to deflect attention from herself. She knew that the criticism she levelled at the well known healers was the same as the one she most feared for herself: that they might become cult figures; that the charisma which comes with the charismatic gift of healing could overshadow the grace which their healing hands were merely channelling. She knew herself how easy it was to begin to see oneself in the two-dimensional status of a 'personality'; the comfort which other people's attention brought. The same people for whom she had such respect could display an unnerving propensity for devotion to a tangible personality rather than an unseen God to whom such thanks was really due.

Gilbert Shaw had often talked of the close bond between the demonic and the spiritual. He had recounted the story of Lucifer to her on several occasions and always reminded her that Lucifer had been an angel. The images of the story so accurately illustrated his experience of the invisible line of temptation which could catapult the search for holiness into an unholy abyss. Sin seemed to be directly linked to knowledge of God: the more closely one understood the path of the Lord, the more likelihood there was of falling away from that path. Any human being who has been given an insight into the way of the Lord is no less human; and therefore their burden becomes the greater. Sin is knowing what is right and yet not doing it. To know what is right is not the same as to be able to live what is right; hence Gilbert's emphasis on self-discipline through prayer. Only by placing oneself squarely within a demanding framework of prayer is there any hope of safe-guarding oneself from the accompanying dangers which such insight brings.

The dangers of which Gilbert Shaw had talked were the very same that Noel had come across so regularly in her own work. To be given the gift of insight brings with it the responsibility of using it for the glory of God. Like the prophets, you have been granted an understanding of God's will and an ability to express it to people. That is a gift which is astonishing in itself. Couple it with the charismatic gift of healing, and whenever you speak your words will be treated with the utmost seriousness. At least, they will by the laity. Perhaps because of the power which such clarity of thought and word effects, perhaps because they know the dangers which such gifts bring, the leaders of the Church may always be suspicious. The obvious danger is that the awe and adulation with which some can treat such insight leads to conceit and vainglory: a rapid descent into the lust for recognition from our fellow humans rather than from God. More discreet, and therefore more dangerous, is the power derived from so many putting their trust into one person. The examples of those whose humanity had got the better of them (Gilbert would not have been afraid to attribute it to a supernatural force of insidious evil) were there for all to see. What Noel now realised was that the same temptations were there for anyone involved in the healing ministry; albeit in the diluted form of petty jealousy and in-security. It was the more revealing since her own experience had increased her awareness of these everyday emotions as the root of so many afflictions and diseases. The theological link between these and the disruption caused to God's intended harmony and wholeness for creation was not difficult to make. When she prayed these matters through, she came away with new understanding of Jesus' ministry as the salve for broken lives and wounded hearts.

She continued to travel regularly as requests for her help

came in; usually within a local radius, but once or twice a week she made the journey north as far as Marlborough or Trowbridge. For these individual visits she continued to use the Guild of St Raphael liturgy and to work with the parish priests. With her own husband frequently confined to hospital, she was surprised to find that much of her work was taken up with hospital visits and those unable to leave their beds for a church service. God had a way of answering prayers with what was needed rather than what was desired. As she struggled to cope with James' debilitating heart problems, she was introduced to an increasing number of people who were suffering from life-threatening and terminal diseases. Sitting by their beds she was struck yet again by the fact that God's healing appeared to be a three-way dynamic: as she listened and talked with those who were ill, God's grace was already at work, restoring and renewing not only the sick person but also herself. The exhausting nature of the work, the travelling and the constant exposure to misery and suffering were always balanced with the extraordinary strength and courage she witnessed and the hope that they gave her. It was in her nature to want to escape to the retreat of mystery which the silence of contemplative prayer offered her, and to have been directed by two of the country's greatest teachers of prayer was a privilege. For many years she had wrestled with the desire to become a nun; only her daughter had kept her rooted in the nitty gritty of daily life. Now it seemed that her earliest desire to be a doctor was returning and she welcomed the chance for regular contact with a vast spectrum of people. Armed against her own pride and fear with a daily office of prayer, she found enormous strength from the people she met and worked with.

At the same time, she became involved with an exciting new venture in the Marshwood Vale. The Reverend Percy Smith had recently returned to England from Hong Kong and had bought Pilsden Manor with the intention of establishing a home for alcoholics and the homeless. He and Noel had met and talked about healing, which he believed was an essential part of the ministry he was conducting. It was his plan to hold healing services for the individuals he brought into the Pilsden community and Noel was able to suggest possible patterns for such services. She did not involve herself directly with them, but agreed to meet with some of the residents and talk with them.

The closest hospital which dealt with cardiology was Exeter. James was fitted with a pacemaker and spent protracted periods of time under supervision. Noel frequently made the drive to see him, combining it with work when she could and excusing herself from her duties when she couldn't. The drive each way took two hours, and although the improvement to his health which the pacemaker afforded was encouraging, the distance, in case of emergency, was too far. In 1977, when Caroline was considering moving house, the family gathered for their last holiday in Dorset to discuss a move which would bring James closer to the health care he needed, and the whole family together. His pension barely covered living expenses and Donald had never been granted a pension, despite being posthumously decorated for bravery. It was time to sell their house and move somewhere much smaller. Looking at the map, they realised that only one place fitted the bill. After twenty years in the service of its diocese, Noel would finally move to Salisbury.

'HERE AM I – FREELANCE HEALING AT EIGHTY'

20

SALISBURY: A SHIFT IN EMPHASIS

Though night still covers the earth, and darkness the peoples,
Above you the Holy One arises, and above you God's glory
   appears.
               A Song of New Jerusalem, from Isaiah 60

It is only when change happens suddenly that we can recognise
it enough to correct it or analyse its effect on us. Most change
is a gradual process. Too many decisions in life happen as a result
of not deciding. Events take place around us and we cope, rarely
feeling in control enough of the circumstances to make a choice.
If all life is from God, then it behoves Christians to be detached
enough from the stream of life to understand what is happening
and take charge; in order that each day may be lived for the
good. This is why Gilbert Shaw believed so passionately in the
discipline of regular daily prayer and contemplation: it allows
Christians to watch over their lives and order events as they
happen. It also gives people the chance to confess when things
get on top of them and gives them the freedom to begin again.
Accepting the frailty of the human will, it offers the framework
of support and a source of strength to cope when people fail to
live up their own ideals.

   Noel had quickly thrown herself into the old pattern of
answering individual calls for healing, and travelling to those
who called for her. She had wrestled with her marginalisation
by the Church and decided to accept it as her lot. What was

difficult to deal with was the instinct it had created in her to avoid what was happening in the mainstream. She had decided not to join the healing ministry of her local priest, thereby reinforcing her solitary position; but it had been an active choice. Within a very short time of her returning from abroad, she had re-established the pattern of her life, albeit one which was now more isolated. James' illness both reinforced this and took up a great deal of her mental energy. The result was that she withdrew from many of the people she had previously relied on and began to rely only on herself. This was not an active choice. It happened subconsciously and over a period of time.

In her first year in Salisbury, Noel considered the question of her recommissioning carefully. With the arrival of a new bishop she was surprised by her own reticence when deciding how best to approach him. At what point had this begun and from what did it spring? Fatigue? Indifference? Fear? She decided that it was important to first establish herself locally, as she had done on her return from Sark, so that she would have something tangible to offer the Bishop.

After Bath, Caroline had moved to Oxford to study art. She later married and had a family. When she had lived in Oxford, Caroline had instinctively been drawn to the contemplative worship of the Cowley Fathers and taken her daughters to the monastery every Sunday. She had rarely joined her mother on the visits to Fairacres as a child, but worship for her had always meant creating a space to wait on God. It seemed that the love of plainsong and contemplative prayer had been indirectly passed on. On their move to Salisbury, Cathedral worship seemed to offer the best continuity. Noel joined them, when James was not in hospital, fascinated to be at the hub of the diocese. She felt at home in the Cathedral; the vast beauty kept her in touch with a transcendent God, while the spectacular music reconnected her to God without the necessity of using words. In such an enormous building, with a disparate and fluctuating congregation, she was able to achieve the balance of anonymity and community which she preferred. She was not known by any of the Dean and Chapter for her healing ministry, but became a familiar face as the grandmother of a new family.

Once again, people who were sick found their way to her. She had made no effort to get in touch with any of the Salisbury clergy who knew her, nor advertised her presence in any parish magazine. In direct contrast to the failure of the lay Order she had tried to set up in Chideock, she had not had a shortage of work since she was commissioned by Bishop Anderson. It did not seem to matter where she moved to or what else was happening in her life, the people continued to find her. In the first instance, those who called her were from Salisbury itself. She relished the chance to walk to their homes, getting to know the city's well-ordered medieval streets. Once again, she felt called to work at the hospital and began to build up a regular ministry among some of the patients there. Combined with her own visits to James, she became quite a well known figure on the wards of the Infirmary.

Outside the hospital, her work meant that she came to meet almost every parish priest in the city. Whenever she was contacted by someone, she would ask for their address and check the map for their nearest church. Turning to the telephone directory, she would then ring the priest and introduce herself. During this time she became aware that the healing ministry was no longer something which required careful explanation. Nor did it seem to produce the same hostile reaction as it had done in the past. The same sea-change she had noted in Dorset was also established in the city, although she did not yet come across any regular healing services. It was hardly a metropolis, but being in Salisbury gave her the same buzz she had had in London: it was the excitement of being at the centre of things. She had worked for so long in the outskirts of the city, had come to know her diocese as intimately as anyone could. Now here she was at the centre of it all. Everything was connected here; each person extended the network and introduced her to another dimension of the city's life. Here, when you worked with one priest at a healing service, you could be put in touch with another just down the road in a matter of minutes. The prejudice of the separate

137

villages who knew of no-one beyond the village next door was unknown here. It was true that the same tight-knit community of the village was missing, but neither was there the splendid isolation of London. You could walk from church to church and feel part of a network that was easily accessible. The potential for co-operation, and therefore extended influence, was extraordinary.

She soon found that she worked particularly well with one or two priests. Giles Clayton was vicar of a small parish on the old city walls of Salisbury. The worship at St Martin's was more high church than most and he liked the liturgy of the Guild of St Raphael. He was happy for Noel to call him in to work with people who were not closely allied to their parish, and enjoyed the chance to hold small individual healing services. Noel, on the other hand, appreciated the chance to work with a dedicated parish priest who took every care to follow up the services with home visits. Many of those who had arrived at her door with no strong Christian convictions and certainly no history of churchgoing, found themselves very gently welcomed into a new community. This, Noel believed, was the greater part of the healing process: the chance for people to feel part of something and to meet new friends. Increasingly, over the past few years, those who had contacted her had not been regular churchgoers, nor felt attached to any one church community. She recalled her time spent with Brother Edward and the Village Evangelists; how her healing gift had been discovered in the heart of a ministry which was calling people back into God's community. It seemed peculiar that God had seen fit to keep this message so close to her heart and such an important part of her ministry while she herself remained very much on the fringes of the church. Yet now in the late 1970s, as people were becoming increasingly unused to church, she was still drawing them back there, still talking of the same things, in the same way as she had in Camelford and Eggbuckland. The people with whom she talked were not much different either. Their conversation was still full of the anxieties of everyday life which crowded out the space they might otherwise have given to God. Noel would always listen for far longer than she spoke. To have the space to be heard was as much what people needed today as it had been twenty years ago. She reported their concerns and criticisms of the church to those with whom she worked regularly; Gilbert had seen her role as a kind of bridge between the people and the priests, and she continued to fulfil that. She did not want to preach to those she met, but she always made it clear that she worked alongside priests and in churches, whenever circumstances allowed. She found that her stories of Christ's healing were no less important to people, but they were less known. There was still the desire to talk about God and faith, but the discussion was less and less informed. Her own experiences of the Church as institution did not quash her belief that the Anglican Church, at the heart of every parish in the land, had a crucial role to play at the centre of the community. The fragmentation of social groups which had begun after the war, and been recognised by Brother Edward, continued apace. But for as long as the churches stood at the centre of people's homes and the priests had a mandate to visit every British citizen as a member of his parish, the Church had unique access to the heart of the problem.

At the same time as her ministry took her around the length and breadth of the city, she noted that living in Salisbury meant that people were now beginning to turn up at her door. This was a new departure and one which she welcomed. Certainly it allowed her to spend more time with them and to get to know them better. It also allowed her more time to herself: as they left, it was they who were on the move, not she. For a few moments she could remain still and reflect on the person, their circumstances and her next move. This made a surprising difference to her ministry. With such time for quiet reflection and prayer, she felt that she had got her priorities right. However, she was also aware of the potential dangers. Now there was no immediate need to phone the parish priest before she met the person who had called her. There was the temptation to let the visit to her home become the whole of the ministry: particularly when the person was neither a worshipper nor a Christian. This could lead to the focus being put purely on Noel, rather than her gift: something she had been warned of in her training and had always tried to avoid.

At such a point, she knew that what she really needed was a spiritual director who could oversee her prayer life and help her to make sure that her ministry was running along orthodox lines. Once again, she felt the loss of Gilbert and Mary Clare keenly. After talking with some of the priests with whom she had worked, Noel felt that she must centralise her ministry within the church. It made sense that the best place to do this was the central church of the diocese.

21

WORKING WITH DOCTORS

Your love, O Lord, for ever will I sing, From age to age my mouth will proclaim your faithfulness.

Psalms 89:1

Remembering the supportive framework of prayer and discipline which her teachers and directors had always recommended, Noel decided to look more closely at the health of her own spiritual life. In the Cathedral she now had privileged access to some of the most inspiring worship and preaching she could hope for. And so she set out to incorporate one of the daily services into her own office of prayer and worship; be it the quiet calm of morning prayer, the tranquillity of choral evensong or the full splendour of a sung Eucharist.

At each service she attended, Noel prayed that she might be shown a way of involving herself more with the congregation, in a way which fitted in with her ministry. It was not long before she felt she had been given the answer: to establish a contemplative prayer group at the heart of Cathedral worship. She invited some of those whom she knew to talk about the possibility of such a venture, and was surprised by the warmth of response to the idea. A few discussions with the clergy was all it took to co-ordinate a weekly prayer group in the morning chapel. With an advertisement in the newsletter and very little fanfare, it began. Following the pattern of her training, Noel explained the nature of contemplative intercession and the role it could play at the heart of a believing community. Thereafter, the meetings were entirely silent. Each member received a list of those to pray for, and all entered and left in complete silence. There was not a great number of regular attenders, and most were older women like herself, but it felt right that such a group had been established; a pool of silence amongst the efficiency and bustle of that great building. Today, so many years later, it serves the same purpose.

Soon after she set up the contemplative prayer group, a new Dean was appointed to the Cathedral. Despite watching him celebrate the Eucharist several Sundays in a row, and hearing his name on different occasions, Noel did not remember that they had met before. One of the earliest introductions Hugh Dickinson had had to the Church's healing ministry was a small healing service with Noel at the parish where he was a curate in Melksham, some thirty years previously. Since then, he had become actively involved with the same ministry in his parish in Bedford. By the time he came to leave the parish and take up his new position at Salisbury Cathedral, he was convinced of the place of healing within the community and its enormous importance for the renewal of the Church. His intention now was to get a feel for the people in the cathedral community and their interest in establishing healing as part of their worship and life.

Excited at the prospect of a healing ministry centred at the heart of the diocese and of offering a place where people could come for healing services and prayer, Noel accepted the invitation to join a healing group in the cathedral. The idea behind the services they held was that they should be as much like a normal cathedral service as possible, with hymns, readings and a sermon. They would be advertised throughout Salisbury and open to anyone who wished to come. Towards the end of the service, those who wanted to could come up to the altar and one of a team of people would ask about their illness before laying on hands. The priest was part of this team, but it was always the Dean's belief that the priest should in no way be the focus of those who laid on hands. The healing ministry showed no partiality between clergy and laity: and he knew that the number of laity with the gift of healing outweighed the number of clergy. It was also his belief that far more people had the gift of healing than had previously been thought. It seemed to him that it was rather like dowsing: the BSD reckoned that 70% of the population *could* dowse but that only 8% had discovered the talent. Part of the Dean's vision for the renewal of the Church through healing was to show people what access they could have to the spirit of God, if they but asked. He knew that there were those in the Church who had a charismatic gift, whose results were such that they could not be denied, but he also knew that healing could be an arbitrary affair and that it often seemed to happen by degrees. There were always a few who were miraculously healed, but the majority were not. Instead, they were shown a new direction or given hope; their minds were eased or their closest relationships renewed. This was what happened most often. The Dean felt sure that the healing ministry was far wider than first thought; that it extended to every Christian who was prepared to listen to God and offer themselves to their fellow brothers and sisters. Thus the radical pattern for the ministry in Salisbury was established: a group of laity who met together for prayer before every service and who then took the lead at the service itself.

It seemed to Noel a great paradox that during this time of renewal and inspiration at the Cathedral, her own life should increasingly be taken up with the deteriorating health of her husband, James. Early in 1977 a lump on the ribs had been diagnosed as cancerous. Since their move to Salisbury, the cancer had been spreading slowly and irreparably. Noel continued her work in the parishes and hospitals and had found warmth in her friendships among the hospital staff. She understood why so much of her work was now with the hospitals and, in particular, that God seemed to be leading her towards the terminally ill. She could not shut out the fact that James was dying and acknowledged that she was being offered the chance to confront it. She knew that her instinct would have been to run from it and, in her prayers, to ignore it rather than allow God to fail in answering her futile requests for James' health.

143

She had learned through bitter experience that the charismatic gift of healing is not the same as the ability to perform miracles on demand. It is simply a particularly clear channel to God; but God is sometime extraordinarily capricious. She was terrified of praying for James because she felt her discernment of what to pray for was entirely clouded by her emotional desire to have him recover.

When he died in January of 1982, she found conversation with God impossible. In the immediate loneliness of the months that followed she could only sit and offer her numb heart to the emptiness in which she had first known God. She found comfort in the people who continued to come to her and ask that she might lay hands on them. The grace they received was witness to the fact she was not abandoned.

If it were possible to consider such things in the depths of grief and pain, Noel managed to draw comfort from the fact that God had always taken each appalling thread and created the beginnings of a pattern of hope and future promise from the confusion. It was James' illness that had brought her at last to Salisbury; and his prolonged stays in hospital that had allowed her to develop her work in the hospital and the hospice. During this time she had won the respect and admiration of many of those who treated James and the other patients on the cancer wards, and had even enjoyed a few heated discussions with them on the subject of the relationship between healing and the medical profession. But it was with the family's GP that she had the most opportunity to talk; and it had been in the context of James' illness and death that her healing ministry had first been broached. As she coped with her husband's slow death, she found an opening to talk about her work.

Noel had always had great respect for the medical establishment. At the age of eighteen she had wanted to train as a doctor — and would have done so had it not been for her father's belief that well-bred young women didn't do that sort of thing! The only doctor whom she had come to know well was Dr Westlake, the chairman of the BSD. It did not come easily to talk to her GP about healing, but after he expressed an interest in the subject she found the confidence to ask if she might refer some of her patients to him. To her surprise, he agreed, on the condition that he could do the same. And so it happened that when the occasion demanded, Noel would refer some of her cases to her doctor rather than to one of the priests with whom she worked.

During this lonely time immediately after James' death, Noel was assisted by another friend from the IRM, Dr Sister Tressie. Tressie was a nun with the French Catholic Order of La Retraite who had come to England from her native India at the age of nineteen to train as a doctor at Bart's Hospital, London. She had come from a pious Catholic background and found herself considering taking Orders during her training. Once qualified, she made investigations and found she would still be able to continue to practice as a doctor if she joined La Retraite. She brought to the Order both a rich history of eastern spirituality and a brilliant young mind. When she met Noel she was already in her late seventies. The two women met every week and spent long hours talking, praying and laughing together. Their conversation covered all aspects of healing and Noel was particularly interested in Tressie's knowledge of Indian influences on contemplative prayer. Sister Tressie had been directed by the Jesuits for some years and introduced Noel to the work of Ignatius Loyola and other great writers in the spiritual tradition, including the rather more unorthodox work of Anthony de Mello. That there could be such an international mix of influences in one person appealed to Noel, who was tremendously grateful for the support and religious input which Tressie gave.

22

HEALING IN SALISBURY: A NEW EXPERIMENT

Give us wisdom to perceive you, diligence to seek you, patience to wait for you, eyes to behold you, a heart to meditate upon you and a life to proclaim you.

Prayer of St Benedict

In working alongside doctors, Noel felt at last that she was working as she had always wanted to: in partnership with the medical establishment. The Church had long since recognised the need for working in such partnership and Dorothy Kerin, in particular, had seen it as imperative. However, at an institutional level the dialogue was irregular and unsatisfactory. Although the circumstances were entirely different, Noel even felt the same security of vision and affirmation that working with Gilbert had given her. She was both learning and teaching. Now she was also learning about symptoms, remedies and side effects. In turn, she was able to throw light on a much wider perspective of health and healing. But if James' death opened the way to new friendships and a new co-operation with doctors, it also offered her the chance to think deeply about the future direction of her healing ministry. With the establishment of a permanent healing group at the Cathedral, she had to decide if God wanted her to incorporate her own distinctive pattern of ministry fully into their new venture, or whether she should also concentrate her energy on the steady stream of people God was bringing to her door. In 1983 she had been asked by the Bishop to work alongside a newly appointed diocesan adviser on healing, the Reverend Ken Brown[34]; another possible direction for her ministry. In that year after James' death she felt both inspired by her contact with the doctors and exhausted by the possibilities which now seemed to be opening up for her. So she decided to take up the offer to make use of a friend's holiday home in Lanzarote for an extended period of retreat and research.

Noel thought that her time should be spent considering carefully what her healing ministry had been about thus far, and where it was going in the future. Particularly inspired by her work in the hospitals and the hospice, she had a gut feeling that she must pursue the question of science and medicine; and it seemed to her that the best way to begin to understand a subject was by looking at its definition. So, she took with her fifteen dictionaries which ranged in subject from genetics to geology, electronics to natural history and psychoanalysis. She felt sure that there was a connection somewhere between the various strands of her life and therefore also between these various disciplines. In her heart she was certain that the connection lay in God and healing, but there were still too many questions left unanswered. The plan was that she would do her research and then write up her findings as an article (perhaps for the BSD or a theological journal). In dedicating the latter part of her life to healing, Noel had been dogged by one intellectual conundrum: the question of where religion meets science. She had been involved with the dowsing society, learned about radiesthesia, and worked with doctors – but she still felt no nearer to the truth. The truth, for her, was a matter of discerning the thread which connected all these together and perhaps, at the same time, discovering a 'middle way'.

Why should God be ceaselessly battered with the prayers of some and thereby ignore those who didn't know how to ask? In a situation where a woman is terribly ill and in need of an operation, should it be a question of *either* praying *or* having an operation? If one followed the logic of some of the charismatic healers of the American evangelical tradition who were receiving so much coverage in the 1980s, prayer should be enough.

The middle way was to do both; as well the Anglican tradition knew. What so few people seemed to be concerned with, however, were the implications of this for the relationship between the medical and religious professionals. Why should God be bothered with apparently trivial illnesses? Why had humanity been given rationality and extrasensory perception? Did these gifts not come with the responsibility to use them whenever possible? If so, what of prayer and healing? Where do they fit in? People had only ever come to Noel when the doctors could do no more. Should healing be left for the urgent cases only? Should it be there to fill in the gaps which medicine could not yet fill? Or was Christianity entirely separate from all this? Was healing concerned only with the spiritual health of a person? She knew better than that! For her, God had always been entirely caught up in the world and its concerns, while also utterly transcendent of them. Maybe this, then, was the dialectic she was dealing with: the involvement of God with the created order on the one hand and the autonomy of humanity on the other. So many questions! If she had had access to a mind like that of Gilbert Shaw or Mary Clare at this juncture she would probably not have left the shores of England for her answers. But it seemed that there was no-one she knew any more with whom she could talk. Where were the scholars? Where were the theologians to chart and monitor this dramatic explosion of the healing movement in the Church? Was it that the days of her contact with the thinkers and the writers were over, or was it that there wasn't anyone thinking and writing about it? Perhaps if she had been in her forties and not in her seventies she would have decided to retrain as a doctor. But as that option was not open to her, she went to Lanzarote, on a personal mission to try and tie up some of the many threads of her life and discern what shape God wanted her ministry to take in the future.

23

HEALING IN SALISBURY: AN OVERVIEW

Finally, let us never forget that there is a spiritual power to heal which has not been withheld. It has only been unappropriated. The slow development of our spiritual receptivity and insight hinders the recovery of thousands who could be healed.

Dr L Weatherhead,
Psychology, Religion and Healing[35]

Archive material documenting the rise of the healing movement in the twentieth century at a national level among the British churches, is no longer hard to find. The importance of the summaries which exist is that they give a sense of cohesion and development to what can otherwise seem a random and unconnected series of events, led by an enthusiastic minority. The weakness of such a perspective is the impression sometimes given of the movement as part of an inexorable march, spearheaded by the determination of a Holy Spirit who knows its time has come. A more accurate picture may be found in the material which gives an insight into the impact of this movement at a local level. That the healing movement was given a charter by an archbishop gave an unknown and uncontainable subject some credibility, but it should not be forgotten that some years after this, one woman was being advised by her spiritual director that her mission as a charismatic healer was primarily to educate. Healing was not touched upon in clergy training, nor widely talked about, except as 'sensationalism'. The Churches Council for Health and Healing and the Guild of St Raphael were neither well-known nor well-supported. Yet, in the dioceses ventures were being undertaken of which Bishop Anderson's experiment was only one. Like Noel's, most of these ventures received no public recognition, no explicit diocesan support, and were not in any way centralised by councils or guilds. In the best tradition of the church, they made their mark at an individual level in small communities. They needed no publicity; their success spread the word and demand never ceased.

It would not be difficult to formulate an argument for the benefits of such an approach to healing in the church. However, one cannot ignore the dangers of a ministry which exists almost entirely at the level of experience and naturally resists any attempt to rationalise or systematise it. The power of healing is not disputed. In his commentary on the healing ministry, Bishop Morris Maddocks talks of 'unleashing the power of healing'. The phenomenal capacity for healing to transform and renew is unparalleled in the Church, so raw is the energy behind it. Gilbert Shaw was the person who alerted Noel to the potential which a fallen race has for corrupting such absolute energy. It was he who understood the intimate association of evil with good. Jesus's healing ministry was as much about exorcising evil as it was restoring good health. Christ himself warned that there would be false messiahs with the power to heal: it is a gift which seems to be connected at a most profound level with God's creation and which cannot therefore be restricted to those who follow Christ. Those Christians who have the gift are beholden to use it in His name, but the power is not exclusively theirs. These are reasons enough for the Church to fear the healing ministry, and fear may be an appropriate response to such overt examples of the power of God and the corruption of humanity. In biblical terms, however, fear of the Lord was never equated with paralysis. Agreeing to do God's work is a risk, it requires necessary humility; but armed with the promise of prayers answered, it is a risk which has to be taken. By

150

setting up an official Council, Archbishop Temple was hoping to offer some reassurance to his sceptical brothers. In the final analysis, however, all bishops were free to make their own choice about the management of healing in their own diocese.

Salisbury took the initiative as early as the 1950s — when Bishop Anderson discovered Noel, trained her and gave her the freedom of the diocese. However, the experimental status of the project, the lack of funding, and a fire at the Bishop's residence which destroyed all records, meant that after Anderson's retirement the initiative lay with Noel and the enthusiasm for healing of successive bishops. Although she was never discouraged from healing, neither was she actively supported. During her work, she had built up links throughout the diocese and knew by first name all those priests and prominent laity who were interested in healing. In one person it was possible to find all the centralised information that any bishop wanting to follow the lead of William Temple would have needed. However, it was not until Anderson's experiment had been under way for thirty years that a group of interested priests was granted the audience of the presiding Bishop of Salisbury, John Austin Baker. Their intention was to establish a regular, official forum for support, encouragement, fellowship and information sharing on the subject of healing. The Bishop invited them to hold an inaugural meeting in the South Canonry in November 1982. Fifty priests attended, more than twenty sent their apologies and requested that they be included in the future. The number alone would have been enough to gladden the heart of a woman whose mission had once been described as 'to convert the clergy'. However, by restricting the meeting to the ordained, the meeting was unrepresentative in not hearing the voices of women and laity; those at the meeting were deaf to the very channels through which the spirit was working.

However, the minutes of that meeting bear witness to the impact of Noel's personal ministry and training on many of those with whom she worked. Her own concerns were echoed on several occasions in a programme which covered personal ministration, public services, deliverance and inner healing. Each of the four speakers emphasised the need for one-to-one listening and prayer. Reverend John Whetten talked of four-hour individual sessions with those who had asked for help, repeated for anything up to six months. This allowed time when two people could pray and read scripture, where hands could be laid on the person asking for healing, but most of all where that person could be listened to and given encouragement. The necessity of co-operation with medical practitioners was stressed, for personal links with local doctors and psychiatrists. It may have been Noel's conversations with Ken Brown which alerted him to the fact he raised, that 80% of those who made use of the healing ministry in the diocese of Salisbury were 'unchurched'. The same was true for those who came to public services.

The meeting was a great success for those who had attended and it was agreed that there would be a diocesan meeting for clergy on the subject, every year. The Bishop also agreed that there should be local meetings which the laity could attend. In fact, the annual meeting did not become a fixture, and from this point on the committees began to run themselves. At diocesan level, the Bishop's Advisory Committee on Health and Healing was established. This committee was made up of eight members; one adviser and one convener from each of the archdeaconries of the diocese. Using the Bishop's own definition, 'the purpose of the Advisers is two-fold: to advise the three Bishops on any matters connected with the Ministry of Health and Healing, either points referred to them or points which they feel the Bishops ought to take on board, and to advise the clergy and parishes on such matters as Healing services, study courses etc., and to organise training and discussion sessions, e.g. between doctors and the clergy'. It seemed that the role of the conveners was intended to be more administrative in taking 'responsibility for such matters as organising training days, circulating information to clergy etc'. In practice there would be little to distinguish the two roles, but having two people from each area gave them mutual support.

Each of the four committees then established a local group, which included the experienced and enthusiastic laity, and would feed into the Bishop's Advisory Committee. It took several years for both diocesan and archdeaconry committees to establish themselves. With a clean page, they had to decide what their role was to be, the scope of their possible goals, and the number of meetings it would take to achieve these. It was not until 1987 that Noel was invited by an old acquaintance (who had since become the Bishop's Adviser, for Sarum) to join the newly formed Sarum Archdeaconry Committee for Health and Healing. It was with some trepidation that she did so: after thirty-five years of solo ministry, it felt quite alien to be sitting on a committee for healing. Her fellow members made it easier for her to consider the prospect: all of the laity who sat with her were women. Those four priests who made up the rest of the committee were all men she knew and had worked with. David Slater, the dynamic priest at Bulford to whom she had been introduced by her friend Lady Camilla Beresford Peirce, chaired the meetings. He had already organised one tremendously successful teaching week on healing at Bulford and was planning an 'advanced' week. After a tentative start, the meetings were scheduled to be quarterly. The agenda for the next one was full with ideas for training courses and counselling days.

This, indeed was how they were to continue. The Archdeaconry Committee became increasingly important in planning the training of both clergy and laity. Speakers were brought into meetings to discuss such subjects as the abuse of drugs and tranquillisers and care of Alzheimer's victims. Yet, within two years, almost every person on the original committee was to resign. The role of the group took time to develop and many of the founding members felt they could not offer what was needed. With each resignation came the opportunity to clarify the committee's aims and criteria for membership. In 1989 the Bishop agreed the request to include at least one doctor on the committee to further their desire for dialogue between healing and the medical establishment. As the Cathedral healing group established itself, membership of the committee reflected the explosion of interest among the Cathedral congregation. While the remit of the committee was never to hold services or to be a prayer or fellowship group, the training days and courses were a great source of help and information for those in the Cathedral healing group.

Noel resigned from the group at the same time as one or two of the other members. Her reasons were concerned mainly with the fact that she would rather spend time in her ministry than sitting on a committee. Her days of training were long since over and while she was happy to help in an advisory role, she did not feel she had much to contribute to meetings.

It was not until 1995 that the diocesan and archdeaconry committees felt that they had significantly raised the profile of healing within the diocese. By this time, Salisbury was being held up as a leading example of a diocese which had taken seriously the charge of the Lambeth Conference of 1988.[36] Crucial to their success was the determination of a few priests that the laity should be given exactly the same encouragement and training as the clergy. More than this, the laity were believed to be the vital resource that they had already proved themselves capable of being. Noel watched in astonishment as the way was opened up for lay people to take up positions of responsibility and authority in the development of the healing ministry in Salisbury. The close connection of the diocese with the Acorn Trust at Burrswood set up by Dorothy Kerin, was initiated by the laity, and it was this Trust which provided such inspiration for Salisbury's training courses and retreats. The newly-established healing group at the Cathedral now consisted almost entirely of laity. Noel's own foundation of the contemplative prayer group completed the network of support for healing which the laity provided.

The length of time it took before healing had the profile and influence it deserved in the diocese proved to be an important part of its development. When, finally, Bishop Baker agreed a date for the first day of Celebration of Healing, he commented

that 'it has been a long time coming, but I myself think that
the delay may have been no bad thing, in that a good deal of
grass roots preparation has been taking place and the ideas are
becoming more familiar'.

24

'. . . THE VOICE OF THIS CALLING'

We trace back til thought fails, the long line of ages through which the earth was prepared to be our dwelling place, but we refuse to accept time as a measure of the soul.
                                B F Westcott, *Christus Consummator*: 22

After her return from Lanzarote, Noel found that the concerns with which she had left England were no longer as pressing as they once were. She had acknowledged the complexities of her profession and learned to rest easy with the questions which had previously consumed her. Today, she prefers to talk of the iniquity of excessive analysis and overactive brains: not because she has transcended this herself, but because she now recognises some of the noise that has been crowding her mind. Healing is not something which can be grasped, nor is it an hypothesis to yield verifiable data. For so long it had seemed possible that its complex nature could be better understood by discovering its relationship to medicine; but thirteen dictionaries, covering every digression of thought, were enough only to clog her mind, spirit and soul with unconnected definitions. She returned with the conviction that holistic treatments from the east were the way that medicine was now healing the fractures in its own discipline, but she was not convinced that her healing experience was an interchangeable sibling in this newly recognised family. While it was true that healing was far wider than the ministry she practised, it was also true that the gift she had been given could not be reduced to its own lowest common denominator. The spirit could not be restricted but it must occasionally be named.

During her time abroad, Noel had attempted to analyse the complicated reality of the healing movement in the Church of England; to understand its history and to trace some patterns for its future. She was excited by the recognition it was now receiving, by its steady move from the fringes to the mainstream; and wondered which part of the mosaic she might have fitted into were she thirty years younger. Perhaps the role of co-adviser to the Bishop was a seemly one now that she was seventy-five. And she knew that if she committed herself to the Cathedral healing group they would carve out a role to suit her, but both options would require her to channel her energy in new directions. As she considered the remaining quarter of her life, she felt an imperative now to build on the foundations God had already given her: her gift for listening in a cell-to-cell ministry and her discipline of prayer and the daily office, both of which flourished as part of her natural inclination to work as a solitary. The one major change that she had to adapt to came about as a matter of necessity rather than choice: her age now seemed to dictate that she terminate her days as an itinerant and base her ministry permanently in one place. Living close to the centre of Salisbury allowed her to focus herself at home.

Although she was now past the age of retirement, she never once found herself out of a job. People continued to come to her door in a steady stream; usually about three people a day. Her time with these people was spent listening and explaining the biblical teaching on healing. She never ceased to be amazed at the results which a few hours of listening to a person could effect. During this time she would ask the occasional questions needed to estimate a diagnosis. Many of those she saw needed only the time and space to talk through their problems, and had resolved to heal the situation themselves by the time they came to leave. Some needed psychiatric treatment, some could be referred on to doctors, and occasionally some needed help to arrange to be taken into a hospice. With those who needed

157

a healing service, she would take more time: seeing them on several occasions so that she could prepare them. She always wanted to make sure that they understood healing within the framework of the faith they had. It was not just a matter of retelling the stories (although that in itself could have an enormous impact). Nor was it a question of trying to explain the intricacies of God's grace and blessing. She did not pray with those who found it uncomfortable to do so, but she wanted to establish an atmosphere of prayer between the person, herself and God: periods of silence and restfulness as they talked. In the meantime she would hold them up to God in her prayers at every office she said.

As she became less able to leave her house, the number of those coming to her increased. She still referred those who needed it to the priests with whom she had worked since arriving in Salisbury, but she herself took part in the services less frequently. Indeed, a point came when her charismatic gift of laying on of hands was barely used. There seemed to be a number of reasons for this: she had never been happy about undertaking this ritual without the structure of a service and the presence of a priest. Even were she to feel entirely comfortable about conducting such a service in her own home, there were far fewer people for whom it was an obvious next step. The need for healing was more apparent than ever, but orthodox Christian belief and practice was becoming alien to a growing majority of those she saw. In such cases, Noel was not always convinced that the ritual of a Christian service would help. It seemed extraordinary to her that at this late stage in her life she should find herself encountering the same anti-church sentiments Brother Edward had sent her to tackle forty years earlier. Then, she had been fired with an energy and enthusiasm which age had since quietened. Her approach now was to listen and wonder and pray. Prayer above all. People were drawn to her home by the oasis it offered them. Often they did not know why it left them rested and uplifted, but they continued to come.

This situation did not change when, as she approached ninety, she chose to move herself from her own home into a nursing home. Perhaps the most important gift that healing had shaped in her over the years was that of discernment. When she reached eighty, Noel had decided that she should give up her car. Those around her were horrified at the loss of independence that this would entail, and her contemporaries found it impossible to understand why anyone would relinquish such a freedom before necessity demanded it. But for Noel, freedom was to be found in strange places. At this time, it was to be found in the dignity which the decision brought: the dignity of having made an independent choice. And with it came new benefits – the chance to walk further, to explore her own corner of the city, to rediscover the local shops, and to meet all the people that this slower, gentler lifestyle allowed. She arranged taxis to take her to Cathedral services and into town for such treats as sale shopping; whilst finding out all about the lives of those who drove her to her destination. Though more stationary than she had ever been, Noel's healing ministry seemed to be growing. And while she could no longer write up all the case notes, she was working for the first time within the context of people she saw quite regularly. The concept of 'follow up' was broadened to include a kind of healing relationship.

No longer did she fraternise with editors, politicians, doctors and the religious, but rather kept the company of those who lived around her and their relatives; the woman for whom the care of her elderly mother had become too much, the young single mother whose child Noel doted on. In each case there was a fractured relationship which was at the root of their unease about life: with everyone she had ever spoken to of healing, this had been the case, right back to the very first people she had helped in Eggbuckland and Charminster. She was quite convinced of the role which human relationships played in people's health and wellbeing. A visit to the elderly mother when her daughter was away, gave them time to share a sherry and some light-hearted banter. She spent time holding the baby for a young woman who had forgotten what it was like to be asked about herself. In this respect, the healing spirit was at its most simple and perhaps its most effective.

What power humans had been given if only they recognised it! As she reflected on it, she knew that when Jesus walked the earth, he brought as much of this kind of healing as he did miracles. It was the latter for which he was remembered as a healer, but she was not certain that the latter was any more important than the former. The charismatic gift of healing had determined her life's work. She had found a silence within herself which had made some sense of her life; she had offered it to God. The commission she received in return was unlike anything she could have expected or requested. Yet had she not accepted it and worked in that capacity for God for forty years, she would not now have had the understanding of that other kind of healing which now characterised her life.

It seemed remarkable to her now that the quest for an intellectual appreciation of her work had taken up so much of her time. She really should have known better! Her work with doctors, however, was something she would always cherish; the discussions between the doctors and priests at the IRM meetings should have continued at least unto the present day: their value had increased with time, not lessened. Perhaps she should have poured more of her energy into maintaining them, or establishing a viable alternative. So much of healing was about relationship, and the relationship between these two professions was crucial to the future of the healing ministry in the church. Neither profession could afford to go it alone; yet she saw little evidence of them doing anything other than pursuing their individual lines of enquiry. But she had never been good at the mindless administration necessary for the buttressing of organisations. She relied on institutions and the structure they provided for her to lead an unstructured life, and so she could never ally herself too closely to them. The closest she had come to putting up the scaffolding before doing the tightrope walk was with the journal she had founded in London. The Church and the medical profession needed a forum for mutual learning. She would love to speak at it, work for it and publicise it, but she was not the type to have established it. The gift old age was bringing her was *time*; time to talk, to listen, to learn about the lives of those she might otherwise only have seen once. The snapshot was becoming a fuller picture – and it deepened immeasurably her ability to heal those who came to her.

When Noel decided to move to the nursing home, her friends were confounded once again. She was disproving all their fears of being abandoned, neglected and waiting to die among the insane. Because, for Noel, the move made perfect sense. She no longer wanted to be concerned with shopping lists and menu planning. Organising the care and upkeep of a home had lost its charm; the fine detail of life which so occupies the mind was now a chore. All she really wanted to do was to withdraw deeper into prayer, and to use the power which those prayers seemed to unleash to heal people. As her own faculties gradually diminished, she decided to allow others to take over the minutiae of life. If her mind was no longer cluttered with anxiety about her health, if she could be woken with a cup of tea and brought three meals a day, then the energy she did have could be used for its most important purpose; to glorify God. And so it happened that at the end of her extraordinary life, she had finally come to live 'in community'; but also as the solitary she always was. In a beautiful corner room, saturated with light from the wide horizons of the Hampshire countryside, she took all her meals alone, spoke only to her family by telephone, and fed her mind with a huge variety of subjects from talking books. But most of all she delighted in the time she had, and the patience her age had given her, to wait on the Lord. For long hours she would sit by her windows, alone with God. Her reading was less academic and more spiritual; she felt she was drawing closer to that which she had for so long seen only 'in part, through a glass, darkly'. Her intellect had been her armour, but now she saw it in battle with the truth, in conflict with the reality she occasionally glimpsed.

And still she was given the chance to change people's lives. Having sold her house and counted her assets, she now had the pleasure of being able to help people financially: a washing machine for one of the nurses who had never had one, the telephone bill of another. The staff came and sat with her –

the laundry mistress, the technician, a young man from the canteen and the teenage cleaner earning money for a gap year. She would listen endlessly to the details of their lives and pray for them.

Healing was more universal, more holistic and more paradoxical than she had ever imagined. There were certain principles which she had derived from her experience, about working with doctors, about theological training. Even these, however, were insignificant when one became caught up in the whole picture. She had always tried to grasp the whole; never been happy with fragments of truth. It had frustrated most of her life, but she felt she was getting closer. In the end she was faced with what she had discovered in the beginning. The silence. The solitude. This is what had been the thread which connected the disparate parts of her life. Always alone: on the fringes: on the move. Never in the thick of the crowd, never fully immersed in the world. Running, instead, along the perimeter trying to figure it all out. Now she was being called to account as a stream of people came to ask her what it was she had seen. Immobilised as she now was in the day-to-day, the community she had side-stepped took her to their hearts. For the first time she was actually involved in the lives of those she met, as fully immersed in the world as she could be. And this was her freedom. She had searched for the overview her whole life; refused to allow herself to be tied to one place or one set of people lest she forget how to fly. What had not made sense to her until now was that it is not the extraordinary which determines life but the ordinary. Everything relates to the mundane. It is not the politicians and the leaders, the astronauts nor the film stars who understand. It is the woman on the street: the one who has loved and borne children, cared for parents and earned enough money to live. Her relationships are what connect her to the underlying reality. That is the power that God has given in creating humanity. The essence of their own salvation; available in the things they take most for granted. The only thing they have forgotten how to do is talk to one another. Should they ever begin to do that again, they might hold the key to their own health; to wholeness.

Noel was still a solitary, in the midst of proximity's gritty realism. It was just that prayer was no longer a space deep within, but a way of living.

> *With the drawing of this Love*
> *and the voice of this Calling*
> *We shall not cease from exploration.*
>   T S Eliot, *Little Gidding*

AFTERWORD

Noel Wynyard discovered the ability to heal during a mission with Brother Edward's Village Evangelists in 1952. She was commissioned by the Bishop of Salisbury in 1955 to heal throughout that Diocese. The number of people who made use of the Bishop's 'experiment' meant that it rapidly became a full-time job, providing work from 1955 until the present day. She has never advertised, nor has she ever been paid.

Without the benefit of independent means, nor the time to take up part-time work, Noel utilised the potential in the expanding property market to finance the project herself. While maintaining an individual ministry, she has consistently worked in conjunction with a parish priest, under the auspices of the Church of England.

FOOTNOTES

1 Editorial. *Life Line, The First.* November 1947 (G Bless 1947–51).
2 Philokalia Kadloubovsky, E & Palmer, G E, *Writings from the Philokalia* (Faber & Faber 1951).
3 *The Woman Who Could Not Die* (Constable 1944). *Flame in the Snow* (Constable 1945).
4 Universities Mission to Central Africa. Merged in 1965 with the Society for the Propagation of the Gospel (SPG) to become USPG.
5 The journal folded in 1951 after printing its thirteenth edition. Instituted to uphold the values of the British Empire, it was faced, at the same time, with the rapid disintegration of the Empire after the Second World War. Noel Wynyard realised that the Atlantic Union was now taking its place in importance and so travelled to the United States of America in 1949 for several months to raise capital for *Life Line* with a slightly different angle on current affairs. When this failed, the *Reader's Digest* offered to buy the journal and run it along their own lines. Noel Wynyard refused and the journal was terminated.
6 In 1904, the Guild of Health was set up by Anglican, Percy Dearmer 'to help people experience within the fellowship of God's family the freedom and life promised by Jesus Christ'. It became interdenominational in 1915 and the specifically Anglican Guild of St Raphael was set up at the same time.
7 1958 Lambeth Conference, *Church Commission on the Ministry of Healing*.
8 See Chapter 6.
9 Michael Joseph 1941, *Pastor's Progress* (Faith Press 1958).
10 Bishop Anderson quoted in *The Church's Ministry of Healing*, article in the *Sarum Gazette*, 9/1955 by Arthur Hopkinson.
11 *Pastor's Progress*, p. 232.

12 Founder of Christian Aid and Secretary for the Churches Council for Health and Healing from 1975.

13 Dr Percy Dearmer, *Body and Soul* (Isaac Pitman 1909). In 1904 this Anglican theologian helped to found the Guild of Health to encourage co-operation with the medical profession in the practice of healing.

14 'There is no rivalry between the sacramental and the charismatic methods of healing *in the Church* (outside the Church there is a rivalry leading to many dangers). This conviction forms the basis of a notable experiment in our diocese which in a very short time of proving has already been the source of many blessings. Mrs Noel Heath (formerly Davidson), of Lifeline House, Chideock, near Bridport, has been authorised by the Bishop to exercise her charismatic gift of healing in any parish to which she is invited by the parish-priest. She is only willing to act in co-operation with him, asking him to join in the Laying-on-of-Hands and the prayers; thus combining both methods or aspects of healing.' Quoted from *Pastor's Progress* p. 234.

15 This and all following quotations taken from the article in the *Sarum Gazette*, ibid.

16 Gilbert Shaw, *The Face of Love* (Mowbray 1959).

17 The resolutions were seen as reason enough not to refer officially to the subject again until the 1978 Conference. See Maddocks, *The Christian Healing Ministry*, pp. 106/107 for further details.

18 Noel and Donald had worked harvesting teak in the forests of Burma for the duration of their marriage before the war broke out in 1939. Between them they managed a herd of elephants and a large team of men. Details of this time are written up in Noel's book, *Winning Hazard* (Samson Lowe 1949).

19 Aubrey Westlake, *The Pattern Of Health* (Element Books 1985) p. 17.

20 Dr Ernest Jensen (Harley Street physician and first doctor in the UK to use a pendulum for diagnosis and treatment), Dr Dudley Wright (surgeon, physician and dietician), Dr Hector Munro and Dr Guyon Richards are considered to be the four founders of the discipline of radiesthesia in Britain.

21 Joseph Fison, Bishop of Salisbury 1963–1973.

22 Dorothy Kerin had also been called to healing and had had to establish for herself the pattern which her ministry would take. She was not attached to one particular church, but by the time she had established the healing centre at Burrswood (1948), the

church there played a vital role in the ministry which she had begun. She always had a priest conduct the services and work alongside her.

23 See Maddocks M, *The Christian Healing Ministry* (SPCK 3rd edition 1995) p. 97.
24 ibid p. 98.
25 ibid p. 98. Reference being made in particular to Ambrose, Augustine, Jerome and Gregory.
26 ibid p. 98.
27 From this came the Emmanuel League of Prayer, an integral part of the later Divine Healing Mission (DHM) which is now tended by the contemplative monks at Crowhurst.
28 It was with Hickson that Gilbert Shaw had first discussed the importance of this aspect of the healing ministry.
29 *The Ministry of Healing* (SPCK 1924).
30 For example, the submission in the 1950s to the Archbishop's Commission on Divine Healing.
31 There is a regular magazine, *Health and Healing*, annual conferences and a training video.
32 See Maddocks M, *The Christian Healing Ministry* (SPCK 3rd edition 1995) p. 164.
33 *Your Very Good Health*, ed. Brian Frost (1980).
34 In 1978, the Lambeth Conference had given its warmest support to the healing movement with Archbishop Coggan inviting the leaders of the churches to appoint representatives of the healing ministry. In 1983, his successor appointed an Anglican Adviser on healing, who began to define his role by holding a series of conferences throughout the country. The bishops were invited to send their representatives to these conferences, with a view to becoming advisers in their dioceses.
35 Published Hodder 1951.
36 *The Truth Shall Make You Free* (ACC 1988) section 1 pp. 47–49. Paragraph 86 (pp. 48–9) states: 'We urge all Bishops to encourage, to oversee, and to be themselves involved in the ministry of healing in their dioceses. The following are some ways of being obedient to our Lord's commission:
    1 to declare that the ministry of healing should be a regular part of the ministry in every congregation;
    2 to encourage intercessory prayer by members of every congregation, remembering our Lord's promise about agreeing together in prayer (Matt 18.19);

167

3 to foster the use of laying on of hands with prayer by the clergy and members of the congregation;

4 to bless and provide oil for the anointing of the sick and to encourage priests to make this anointing a regular part of their ministry;

5 to develop counselling ministries, concerned with inner healing and the healing of relationships, and to provide for the ministry of absolution and the assurance of forgiveness;

6 to provide and oversee ministries of deliverance from demonic oppression where this is needed, and where appropriate, with medical consultation;

7 to establish in each province and/or diocese centres for the ministry of healing, both for the ministry to the sick and for the teaching and support of those engaged in this ministry at the local level;

8 to work in partnership with doctors, nurses and all involved in the care of the sick, and to encourage medical research and the study of related ethical issues;

9 to ask for a fair distribution of resources and personnel so that all nations and all sections of the community may receive adequate health care;

10 to embrace the sick and impaired, for example, drug addicts and sufferers from AIDS as part of the fellowship of the whole Church;

11 to support the Church's medical mission throughout the world as a vital arm of its ministry and outreach;

12 to work for the establishment of hospices for the terminally ill and to provide appropriate ministry for the dying and their families; this will need to include counselling regarding the continuance or otherwise of life-support systems.'

APPENDIX A

OFFICE FOR THE RECEPTION OF AN OBLATE.

The Candidate shall kneel at the Screen in the Chapel.

The Chaplain General or his representative, standing before the Altar, shall say:

In the Name of the Father and of the Son and of the Holy Ghost. Amen.

Veni Creator

Lord have mercy,
Christ have mercy,
Lord have mercy.

Our Father   Hail Mary

Let us pray.

O GOD, forasmuch as without Thee, we are not able to please Thee: mercifully grant that Thy Holy Spirit may in all things direct and rule our hearts. Through ... in the unity of the same Holy Spirit ...

The Priest   addressing the Candidate shall say:

Do you desire to be admitted as an Oblate of the Community of the Sisters of the Love of GOD?

Candidate   I do.

The Priest   shall then ask the approval of the Superior:

Are you willing on behalf of the Community to accept this Candidate as an Oblate of the Sisters of the Love of GOD?

Superior	We are willing.
The Priest	shall then address the Candidate as follows:

The Superior has signified her willingness on behalf of the Community to accept you as an Oblate of the Sisters of the Love of GOD.

Do you promise to observe the Rule prescribed for an Oblate of the Community?

Candidate	By GOD's help I will.
Priest	Will you be faithful in your life and prayer, endeavouring to help and serve in charity those into whose fellowship you are called?
Candidate	By GOD's help I will.
Priest	Will you be watchful for the interests of the Sisters in all your dealings with Externs, observing reticence and reserve concerning the Convent life?
Candidate	I will endeavour to do so always with the help of GOD. I ... hereby offer myself to Almighty GOD and promise by His help to live for the space of one year in faithful obedience to you, Reverend Mother and to those promises which I have made, in the Name of the Father and of the Son and of the Holy Ghost.
Priest	GOD Who has given you a good will, give you also grace and strength to perform what you have promised.

I admit you ... as an Oblate of the Community of the Sisters of the Love of GOD to undertake these obligations for the space of one year: in the Name ...

Blessing of the Scapular

V. Our help is in the Name of the Lord.
R. Who hath made Heaven and Earth.
V. Lord hear our prayer.
R. And let our cry come unto Thee.
V. The Lord be with you.
R. And with thy spirit

170

O GOD, Who hast promised to Thy faithful servants the garments of salvation and the robe of Eternal Glory, we humbly beseech Thee that Thou wouldest vouchsafe to bless this Scapular betokening lowliness of heart: grant that Thine handmaid who is to wear it may ever be mindful of the yoke of our Lord JESUS Christ and of her holy resolve.

Receive this Scapular and see that thou seek so constantly to put on the Lord JESUS Christ that thou mayest ever abide in Him.

Blessing of the Cross

V. Our help is in the Name of the Lord.
R. Who hath made Heaven and Earth.
V. Lord hear our prayer.
R. And let our cry come unto Thee.
V. The Lord be with you.
R. And with thy spirit.

O Lord Jesu Christ, Almighty and Everlasting GOD Who by the will of the Father didst save the world by shedding Thy Blood in Thy Passion on the Cross: bl+ess and hal+low, we beseech Thee, as a sign of Thy Triumph and the Banner of our salvation, this Cross which we conse+crate in love and honour of Thy victorious Name, and grant that she who bears it or looks upon it may be ever mindful of Thy saving Passion, and bear about in her body Thy Dying in the power of Thy Resurrection. Who livest . . .

Receive the Cross of our Lord JESUS Christ as an Oblate of this Community: in the Name of the Father . . .

GOD Who has given you grace to devote yourself more especially to His Service, give you strength to fulfil in your life what you have promised with your lips.

Let us pray

O GOD Who hast prepared for them that love Thee such good things as pass man's understanding: pour into our hearts such love toward Thee, that we loving Thee above all things may obtain Thy promises which exceed all that we can desire. Through JESUS Christ . . .   Amen.

We beseech Thee, O Lord, pour Thy grace into our hearts that as we have known the Incarnation of Thy Son JESUS Christ by the message of an angel, so by His Cross and Passion we may be brought unto the glory of His Resurrection, through the same JESUS Christ our Lord ... Amen.

The Blessing

APPENDIX B

FROM THE BISHOP OF SALISBURY.

—

TELEPHONE: SALISBURY 4031.

SOUTH CANONRY,
SALISBURY,
WILTS.

8th December 1955.

To Whom it may concern

      Mrs. Noel Davidson has my authority
to minister spiritually to the sick, with the
consent of the parish priest in whose parish
the sick person resides.

William Sarum

APPENDIX C

8 December 1955

The Church's Ministry of Healing

Is it a side-line—or does a Pool of Siloam wait in every parish of our diocese?

By the Revd. ARTHUR W. HOPKINSON, Wareham.
An article written at the special request of the Bishop.

There is no prayer for the work of the Church overseas in the 1662 Prayer Book. This omission has been rectified in the 1928 Book. Times have changed. For a hundred years after the Reformation, the Church of England was so much occupied with her domestic affairs that she neglected the divine command, "Go ye into all the world and preach the gospel to every creature." Now, a fresh spirit animates our Church. Missionary work is no longer neglected, or treated as a sideline. For the last two hundred and fifty years, beginning about the time of the inauguration of the Society for the Propagation of the Gospel, the Church of England has evinced a missionary zeal as keen as that of any time since the days of the Apostles. The old-fashioned churchwardens' whimper that "there's plenty of things to spend money on in the parish without sending it outside" is now thank God, a plaint of the past.

But what about the second part of our Lord's commission to His disciples—"Preach the gospel: Heal the sick"? Here again, there are signs of an inspired revival. Churchfolk are awakening to the certainty that Man has a three-fold unity of being—body, mind and spirit—and that the healing of all three is the concern of the Saviour.

174

None of them is a mere side-line in the Church's work. For the Christ who went about doing good and healing the sick is "the same yesterday, and today, and for ever." The revival of divine healing has come two hundred years later than the revival of missionary zeal. But it is none the less important, and none the less real.

It may be said to have begun with the publication of Percy Dearmel's *Body and Soul*, and with the contemporary work of James Hickson, a gifted Church layman, who carried out a world-wide ministry of healing so successfully that those who "came to scoff remained to pray."

It seems a matter of divine providence that these two pioneers should have exemplified, simultaneously, the two methods by which the Church is guided to carry on her Ministry of Healing. Dr. Dearmer emphasised the sacramental nature of the work, its divine sanction in the use of sacrament of Unction, and of the sacramental act of the Laying-on-of-Hands by the accredited ministers of Christ's Church. Mr. Hickson, on the other hand, had a charismatic gift or divine endowment—one of those special *charisma* bestowed upon individuals, of which S. Paul writes in I Corinthians XII 28–31. The fact that the same outward sign of the Laying-on-of-Hands is used in both methods is apt to be confusing, unless it is recognised that they are just methods by which the same truth is exemplified.

In the diocese of Salisbury we are trying to take our part in this great spiritual revival, which is one of the glories of this tempestuous twentieth century. More and more it is becoming recognized that Healing is an integral part of the pastoral work of every parish-priest. Some of us feel that we cannot refuse a candidate for Unction any more than we would refuse a candidate for Confirmation. Whether we consider the candidate suitable for Unction (or suitable for Confirmation) is, of course, quite another matter. For either sacrament some *preparation* is essential. There is still much to be learned; for we are in the experimental stage with regard to this sadly neglected part of the Church's ministry. There is, for instance, the vitally important consideration of co-operation with the Medical profession—a matter in which much happy progress is being made. Those who wish for information and advice in these matters, with a full assurance that it will be in complete loyalty to the teaching of the Catholic Church should apply to The Guild of S. Raphael, 33, Wilton Place, S.W.1, or to its Assistant Chaplain, the Revd. A. H. Purcell Fox, a member of the Churches' Council of Healing and former hospital chaplain, who is Rector of Ashmore, Salisbury, the peaceful village on the Wiltshire-Dorset border, illustrated above, where a Quiet Day was held by the Guild earlier this year.

There is no rivalry between the sacramental and the charismatic methods of healing in the Church (outside the Church there is a rivalry leading to many dangers). This conviction forms the basis of a notable experiment in our diocese which in a very short time of proving has already been the source of many blessings. Mrs. Noel Heath (formerly Davidson), of Lifeline House, Chideock, near Bridport, has been authorised by the Bishop to exercise her charismatic gift of healing in any parish to which she is invited by the parish-priest. She is only willing to act in co-operation with him, asking him to join in the Laying-on-of-Hands and the prayers; thus combining both methods or aspects of healing.

She is not an itinerant magician: and she has thankfully accepted two decrees of discipline—(1) She will not address meetings. Healing, not talking about healing, is her job. It takes the whole of her time. (2) She will not undertake work outside the diocese, partly because her time is fully employed in the diocese, and partly because a wandering ministry often means that the healer works rather promiscuously, having little part in the proper preparation of the patient, or in following-up the case afterwards.

This continuity of ministry, which is best assured by a simple and sincere co-operation in the pastoral work of the parish-priest, is the very essence of our experiment. For the crucial question for everyone seeking healing is—"Why do you want it?" So often the answer must be that it is for some entirely selfish reason. This is a terribly serious matter. The asking of God's help simply and solely for an alleviation of pain, or the removal of some infirmity which is a hindrance to money-making, is unworthy of a Christian. The aim in seeking Healing must always be that we may be enabled to serve God better. Every patient, therefore, needs much help in preparation, and much support later on in the effort to show forth his thanksgiving for healing by serving God better.

This is not an attempt to belittle healing-services, or stirring appeals to crowds, or the efforts of men who re-echo John Wesley's boast, "the world is my parish." It is merely the witness of one, with fifty years of experiment and experience behind him, to what seems to him "the better way."

Reprinted from the special September number of the SARUM GAZETTE, devoted to the Healing Ministry, copies of which can be obtained from the Editor, the Rev. E. B. Brooks, at St. George's Vicarage, Dorchester, price 8d. post paid.

APPENDIX D

SALISBURY DIOCESE
DIVIDED INTO THE FOUR ARCHDEACONRIES
(heavy print)
AND THE DEANERIES

Diagrammatic – not to scale

BIBLIOGRAPHY

On the So-Called Divining Rod or Virgula Divina (Occasional paper for Society for Psychical Research 1897)

Blackie, *The Patient, not the Cure* (McDonald & James 1976)

Chavda M, *Only Love Can Make a Miracle* (Kingsway 1991)

Cobb E H, *Christ Healing* (Marshall, Morgan & Scott 1933. Reprinted 1954)

Curtis G, *William of Glasshampton, Friar — Monk — Solitary* (SPCK 1947, 1978)

de Beausobre, *The Woman Who Could Not Die* (Constable 1944)

Flame in the Snow (Constable 1945)

Fox A H P, *The Church's Ministry of Healing* (Longmans 1959)

Frost B, (ed.), *Your Very Good Health* (1980)

Franksih D, *Radiation, the Best Kept Secret* (Radionic Quarterly Autumn/Winter 1988)

Guirdham A, *The Nature of Healing* (Allen and Unwin Ltd 1964) (signed 1st ed)

Hammond F and I M, *Pigs in the Parlour. A Practical Guide to Deliverance* (Impact Books 1973)

Harton F P, *The Elements of the Spiritual life. A Study in Ascetical Theology* (SPCK 1932)

Hacking R D, *Such a Long Journey. A biography of Gilbert Shaw, Priest* (Mowbray 1988)

Hopkinson, *A Pastor's Progress* (Michael Joseph 1941/Faith Press 1958)

The Church's Ministry of Healing (Sarum Gazette 9/1955)

Horrobin P, *Healing Through Deliverance* (Sovereign World Ltd 1991)

Ikin A G, *Studies in Spiritual Healing. Making Men Whole* (Churches Fellowship for Psychic and Spiritual Study and The World Prayer Fellowship 1968)

Kadloubovsky E and Palmer G E (trans)

Writings from the Philokalia (Faber & Faber 1951)
Early Fathers from the Philokalia (Faber & Faber 1954)
Lambeth Report, *The Ministry of Healing* (SPCK 1924)
The Truth Shall Set You Free (ACC 1988)
Llewelyn R, *Prayer and Healing* (Julian Shrine Publication)
Our Duty and Our Joy (DLT 1993)
Maddocks M, *The Vision of Dorothy Kerin* (Hodder & Stoughton 1991)
The Christian Healing Ministry (SPCK 1981/90/95)
MacNutt F, *Healing* (Hodder & Stoughton 1989)
Rae M, *Radiesthesia and Thought* (paper given at the 1972 Conference
  of the Medical Society for the Study of Radiesthesia)
Shaw G, *The Face of Love* (Mowbray 1959)
Tournier P A, *Doctor's Casebook: in the Light of the Bible* (SCM 1954)
Weatherhead L, *Psychology, Religion and Healing* (Hodder & Stoughton
  1951)
Westlake A, *The Radiesthesic Faculty* (Privately Printed 1973)
The Pattern of Health (Element Books 1964/1973/1985)
Wynyard N, *Durian* (Oxford University Press 1939)
Winning Hazard (Sampson Lowe 1949)
Life Line (G Bless 1947–51)